The P51 Mustang

The P51 Mustang

From Tactical to Strategic Supremacy

Peter Saxton

Pen & Sword
AVIATION

First published in Great Britain in 2024 by
Pen & Sword Aviation
An imprint of Pen & Sword Books Limited
Yorkshire – Philadelphia

Copyright © Peter Saxton 2024

ISBN 978 1 03611 780 1

The right of Peter Saxton to be identified as
Author of this Work has been asserted by him in accordance
with the Copyright, Designs and Patents Act 1988.

A CIP catalogue record for this book is
available from the British Library

All rights reserved. No part of this book may be reproduced or
transmitted in any form or by any means, electronic or mechanical
including photocopying, recording or by any information storage and
retrieval system, without permission from the Publisher in writing.

Typeset by Mac Style
Printed in the UK by CPI Group (UK) Ltd, Croydon, CR0 4YY.

Pen & Sword Books Limited incorporates the imprints of After
the Battle, Atlas, Archaeology, Aviation, Discovery, Family History,
Fiction, History, Maritime, Military, Military Classics, Politics,
Select, Transport, True Crime, Air World, Frontline Publishing, Leo
Cooper, Remember When, Seaforth Publishing, The Praetorian Press,
Wharncliffe Local History, Wharncliffe Transport, Wharncliffe True
Crime and White Owl.

For a complete list of Pen & Sword titles please contact

PEN & SWORD BOOKS LIMITED
47 Church Street, Barnsley, South Yorkshire, S70 2AS, England
E-mail: enquiries@pen-and-sword.co.uk
Website: www.pen-and-sword.co.uk
or
PEN AND SWORD BOOKS
1950 Lawrence Road, Havertown, PA 19083, USA
E-mail: uspen-and-sword@casematepublishers.com
Website: www.penandswordbooks.com

I am grateful for the assistance I received in writing this book from my wife, Barbara, my sister, Kathryn and the ladies of the Winslow Library.

Contents

Chapter 1	A Hesitant Start	1
Chapter 2	Getting Involved	9
Chapter 3	Strategic Bombing	23
Chapter 4	Tactical Superiority – Overlord	31
Chapter 5	Strategy and Politics	49
Chapter 6	On Regardless	59
Chapter 7	Dicing With the Devil	73
Chapter 8	Gaining Altitude	95
Chapter 9	A Fighter with the Range of a Bomber	103
Chapter 10	Air Supremacy	109
Chapter 11	Epilogue	123

Chapter 1

A Hesitant Start

The Second World War in the air was underpinned by several arms races between the combatants to develop the best performing aircraft for use by their armed forces. The British government, in battle joined with Nazi Germany, wanted a single-pilot, single-engine warplane to attack ground forces. The British aircraft industry at the opening phases of the Second World War was distinguishing itself by producing some top-class war planes such as the single-engine Hawker Hurricane, the Supermarine Spitfire, the twin-engine de Havilland Mosquito, the Bristol Beaufighter, and the four-engine Avro Lancaster. There could be no resting on laurels however. What was good this year would undoubtedly be obsolescent within a short time, and the machines in role had to be improved to keep the edge on the opposition or jump to a new variant, preferably using new technological discoveries, that would keep them ahead.

In these so called 'battles of the factories', production and design excellence in themselves were weaponised. There were clear advantages to be gained, for instance, by dispersing this production activity between many companies. In the heavy bomber category

2   The P51 Mustang

spreading orders between three companies – Shorts of Belfast producing the Sterling, Handley-Page producing the Halifax and Avro producing the Lancaster, brought the advantage of reducing the risk that one of the projects might be limited or even fail technically – they had more than one string to the bow. A good example within a single company was Hawkers. In attempting to build a successor to the Hurricane they produced the Tornado model, which was abandoned when the only engine earmarked for it, the Rolls-Royce Vulture, proved prone to failure. However, concurrently they had been developing the Typhoon, already well under way as a project. Unfortunately, this too proved disappointing as it had a fat thickness wing design, which limited its speed at altitude due to the early onset of airstream breakaway. It went into service with the Royal Air Force but as something of a stopgap to those in the know, because yet another project – the Tempest – was also being developed concurrently. The Tempest had a redesigned wing that was thin in depth with a reduced thickness-to-chord ratio and an increased total wing area enclosed within a more elliptical plan form, some of a cluster of developments referred to as 'laminar-flow', of which more anon. Success arrived – the new aircraft did not disappoint and was described as everything the Typhoon wasn't. These separate attempts taken together took some time, but nowhere near as much as if the projects had been managed consecutively necessitating a return to square one each time.

In the heavy bomber arena, British designs delivered some effective service in role. However, the rate of technical development of aircraft in this most innovative of industries meant that they were liable to early obsolescence. The Halifax soon eclipsed the Sterling in its altitude and radius-of-action capabilities. The Lancaster then did the same to the Halifax, so the Lancaster became the heavy bomber of choice as the war wore on, and the whole industry was able to shift to a concentration on further technical development and production of the best machines while abandoning older obsolescent ones.

However, this was not just a question of quality. There was a critical quantitative problem too. Even with the best will in the world and British factories working flat out, it was not possible to guarantee that British output would produce the quantity of aircraft needed. Winston Churchill told the Americans, 'Give us the tools and we'll finish the job!' This was sardonically re-arranged by RAF personnel to, 'Give us the job and we'll finish the tools!'

The British government had set up a liaison committee in New York for the purpose of using the might and versatility of American industrial production to make good the quantity deficiencies they knew were inevitable. The so-called British Aircraft Purchasing Commission was a forum, a market whose officials developed business networks and debated tactical requirements. It was through these channels that, in 1940, officials of North American Aviation (NAA) were drawn into a discussion about a new supply of fighter aircraft for the RAF. The British were interested in acquiring permissions to build the Curtiss P-40 Warhawk. This was not a new design, but a modified version of an even earlier design, the P-36 Hawk, a process that had the advantage of the ability to rush it into production. Designers and board members of NAA, however, championed something more radical.

In early 1940 they submitted a proposal to seize the latest technology by designing a brand-new fighter. They were experimenting with a low-wing monoplane like the Hurricane and the Spitfire, and like those two British aircraft, was driven by a 12-cylinder, liquid-cooled engine manufactured by the Allison Engine Company in the United States. The Allison unit was supercharged, but by a less powerful single-stage unit, which meant that while any fighter equipped with it would perform well at lower levels, performance fell away with altitude, especially above 20,000ft.

The progress on airframe design faced no such impediment. NAA concentrated on experimental data about control of laminar flow. This aimed at a design that facilitated the flow over a wing so that it minimised drag, which meant that the aircraft would increase its top speed and cruise performance for any given power setting. Less fuel flow in the cruise was key – this meant that the aircraft's range performance increased.

They applied themselves to augmenting this advantage in other ways. The engine cooling intake, set far back below the fuselage, was also optimised for the lowest drag possible. It made a further and clever contribution by heating the intake air within the cooling radiator so that it expanded and then constricting its exit from the aircraft using convergent exhausts.

This increased the speed of the expelling air providing a small but significant amount of jet thrust. Named the Meredith Effect after its British inventor, the thrust added some 10–12 mph to the aircraft's forward speed. A similar effect was gained by fitting special exhausts to another aircraft – the de Havilland Mosquito. It was not unique, but it was a savvy bit of development. Taken all together the design added to the aircraft's top speed with commensurate advantage to climb performance as well as range.

In the relentless pursuit of reduced airframe drag, the tailwheel came under scrutiny. All single-engine fighters had fixed tailwheels, i.e. they could not be retracted into the fuselage as could the main wheels and undercarriage legs. At some point someone at NAA must have shown a healthy disrespect for convention and asked, 'Why not?' There was no reason except simplicity. The Mustang was duly designed with a drag-reducing, retracting tailwheel. Other manufacturers quickly followed suit. Small though some of these developments may have been when looked at individually, the gains taken together were critical. Qualitative advantage in war planes are expressed in speed, climb-rates, range (the distances the aircraft would fly on its own internal fuel), endurance (how long you could remain in the air on internal fuel) when compared to your enemies' efforts. The performance of piston-engine fighter planes was now approaching the limits of what this technology could achieve. The closer to that limit each development took you, the more advantage was gained even with relatively small margins of improvement. Taken in this context, even an extra

30mph was thought highly desirable. It was calculated that the new fighter could achieve a maximum speed of nearly 400mph.

Quantitative advantage is expressed in how many of them you can produce and how fast.

There had been admiration expressed for the short time between the British placing the contract with NAA and the roll-out of the first production aircraft, but this achievement was marred by other delays. Technical problems caused the delivery date of the first production aircraft to slip to the end of April 1941, but then NAA, instead of delivering it to the RAF, decided to retain it as a development aircraft instead. The first production aircraft did not reach England until towards the end of the year, a further delay of six months. It was assembled, fitted out, and flown to The Air Fighting Development Unit (AFDU) at RAF Duxford in Cambridgeshire. The test flying there produced a mixed reaction. Inevitably it was assessed by comparison with the Spitfire Mk V. The handling qualities were praised, the stalling characteristics deemed forgiving and the aircraft was swifter than the Spitfire at medium levels. However, the Spit could climb significantly faster and above 20,000ft easily outmanoeuvred the Mustang at all levels. Inferiority at altitude was not acceptable to RAF Fighter Command who remained firmly and justifiably of the conviction that altitude was the key tactic in air-to-air combat and again turned down the possibility of these machines on their inventory. It was sent to the newly formed Air Cooperation Command (ACC), where it would operate within the lower altitudes that its original specification had nominated, for which therefore it was designed, and not surprisingly, where it performed extremely well. The reputation of the Mustang was being prejudiced by attempts to evaluate it in environments outside its design parameters, which in turn had been determined by the British specification requirements in the first place.

The Mustang also attracted little interest from possible United States clients. They were absorbed with improving a suite of American-manufactured existing types, principally Curtiss aircraft, as the main chance. They did, however, obtain two Mustangs which were tested. The American test pilots put them through a programme, wrote favourable reports. And were ignored.

In December 1941, following the gut-wrenching attack by the Imperial Japanese Navy on Pearl Harbour, everything changed. America was now in the war *à l'outrance*. In the scramble to rearm for a massive conflict, the Mustang came back under consideration. It was a ground attack aircraft built for another country but impressed the Pentagon as such, who eventually ordered 500 of this variant. This was more driven by an overwhelming exigency to harness as much manufacturing capacity as possible as fast as possible than being the top contender (that honour went to the Republic P-47 Thunderbolt), but it guaranteed the aircraft's continued existence in some form. Its full potential as a strategic fighter however, remained hidden and unrealised.

Chapter 2

Getting Involved

They started to arrive, these slightly strange-looking new machines. None of the sleekness of a Spitfire, nor the hunched aggressiveness of a Hurricane. This boy looked as if he enjoyed his nights out. From some angles he could appear a bit paunchy.

No 2 Squadron of Air Cooperation Command (ACC) RAF was one of the first to re-equip with this new ground attack aircraft. No 2 Squadron was based at a small aerodrome called RAF Sawbridgeworth, in Hertfordshire. Its neighbours were equally inconspicuous places, but in wartime, inconspicuous is good. Like Great Dunmow, which had nothing identifiably great about it, and Buntingford, said to be haunted by an apparition in white. Strangely, this apparition only ever seemed to appear to people stumbling their way back home from the pub in a fog.

The Second World War largely passed these places by. Even the notoriously quixotic targeting priorities of Luftwaffe High Command had never included an urgency to have a go at Sawbridgeworth. It was an obstacle course just to get to via stopping trains, late connections and taxis. Probably the worst way to get there was in a car down narrow country roads from which all the direction signs had been removed to be as unhelpful as possible to German tanks. The German tanks never came. In the meantime, that one policy must have caused incalculable cost in confusion of movement to the British war effort, especially if you happened to be American, but it was a precaution that was deemed necessary at the time.

Four of the new pilots had, impossibly, crammed themselves into, or were hanging out of, a Riley sports car. One evening, after a hair-raising dash out, swerving around tight corners and nasty potholes, they arrived at a pub called 'The Three Horseshoes' and whooped it up with some enthusiastic local girls. There they were, in RAF uniform, hair long and wavy enough to get the Station Warrant Officer seriously demanding to know what the world was coming to, and with the magic brevet above their left chest pocket. Wings.

Eventually, enthusiastic or not, the eldest of them and the driver of the car, had to get them back to base. He paused while good-night kisses and false promises were duly exchanged. He then led them out from a heaven of huge, longing eyes, curving waists, perfume, and lipstick, into a cold, fog-blind darkness called reality. Driving aimlessly back he got lost. Impossible. So little visibility. So little brain left. Discretion is the better part of inebriation, and the Flying Officer stopped the car, turned the engine off and said the day was lost but tomorrow is another day. They slept. They thanked God, in their befuddled shivering, for RAF greatcoats. The Flying Officer woke four hours later feeling like he had eaten a carpet and looked at the huddled masses. He tried to shout at them, but you can't shout when you've eaten a carpet. So, he turned on the ignition and sounded the horn. It did the trick. The fog had lifted into some very low cloud and the dawn was breaking, as, thankfully, dawns always seemed to do. In a precarious world it was comforting to know that some things at least could be counted on. They arrived back at Sawbridgeworth half-an-hour later.

The armed sentry looked them over, smiled, and said,

'Morning, Sir. Had a good evening?'

'Thank you, Corporal. Not bad, if memory serves.'

'Well, I won't keep you from your breakfast, Sir. Don't think you'll be going anywhere today by the look of that cloud.'

'I'm grateful for small mercies, Corporal.'

'Indeed, Sir.'

The sentry saluted and waved for the gate to be opened. The Riley roared through, all noise and no power. Sounds good though, and that's really all that counts with the girls.

On the following day in less inclement weather, tasked with what might have been one of the first real operational sorties with the Mustang, the senior of the four took off from the tiny strip in the middle of nowhere. The Mustang still had the Allison engine, but this was a medium-level, armed reconnaissance sortie so manoeuvrability at altitude was not going to be an issue. Like the de Havilland Mosquito, whose early bomber marques had teething troubles, tactical and operational experience could be gained by deploying early joiners in technically simpler photo-reconnaissance sorties. The Mustang plied up and down the French coast, centring on Dieppe, taking photographs in preparation for an amphibious raid.

This sortie, and the many other similar ones that followed, were flown under the command of Army Cooperation Command(ACC), a Royal Air Force Command lost in the mists of time. This Command had been formed largely on the initiative of the RAF to ensure the closest and most effective standards of air support for the allied armies. Air Marshal (later Marshal of the Royal Air Force Lord Tedder) was one of a group of powerfully persuasive advocates of integrated, combined operations. They pressed Air Marshal Sir Charles Portal, who was Chief of the Air Staff, to promote a Fighter Command Group to full Command status. Organised into Wing units, each Wing was assigned specifically to an Army Regional Command to provide ground attack to infantry and armoured units, battle area reconnaissance, and fall of shot for the artillery.

They also had the pleasure of being targets for training anti-aircraft gunners. This entailed towing a target drogue for the anti-aircraft gunners to aim at but of course implied that if the trainee gunners applied too much deflection (aiming ahead to hit a crossing target) their streams of shells might creep up dangerously close to the towing aircraft. For a participating pilot, looking down at the firing battery took some self-control.

The tracer shells seemed to curve upwards towards the front of the aircraft and then bend back in an arc. The last few seconds of this could convince you that these shells were aiming directly at your eye. Difficult to be indifferent about that. This was often loudly pointed out by pilots to their Flight Commanders. It rarely raised more sympathy than, 'Well, just don't look down, chum!'

The importance of combining air power to support ground battles – integrated combined operations – was a critical, winning, tactical doctrine that ensured the success of the Allied invasion of Western Europe. It is extraordinary, therefore, that the Chief of the Imperial General Staff (CIGS), General Sir Alan Brooke, should have had such a strong and implacable objection to the ACC. Those opposed to the doctrine believed that the three forces had their own domain to command – land, sea, and air, and mixing them together was unnecessary complication. After all, they insisted, the army didn't try to impinge on sea battles, so why should an air force impinge on a land battle? It was the most extraordinarily narrow logic. They seemed to have been able to ignore the tactical demonstrations of the German invasion of pretty much the whole of Europe. Mobile ground units had advanced behind a barrage of ground attack support in the form of Junkers 87 Stuka aircraft. Stukas and Me 109 fighter-bombers were airborne artillery, used to blast holes in enemy defensive deployments to enable rapid, unopposed advance of armour and ground-holding infantry. But such officers were powerful and had the ear of the even more powerful, as personified in the close relationship between Brooke and Churchill, who referred to him as 'Brookie'. In the Allied invasion of Europe in 1944, the close air support tactics developed in the short life of Army Cooperation Command were essential and decisive.

At about the same time, No 268 Squadron based at Westonzoyland near Bridgwater on the Somerset Levels, was quietly setting new records. The squadron had cut its operational teeth with the P40 Curtiss Tomahawk, a purely American product that had undergone development as part of a suite of Curtiss aircraft. The British Procurement Commission had originally favoured the P40 as a simple off-the-shelf option to boost the RAF's drive for many more fighter aircraft. They were seeking options on delivery of US-manufactured machines, as well as licences to produce and optimise them for RAF use in Britain. It was a surprise therefore that they awarded the contract to the younger North American Aviation, a corporation which had no previous experience in the development of fighter aircraft. There were conditions. The production of the new fighters had to absorb less than a set time and cost ($40,000) for manufacturing each unit and NAA had to produce the prototypes within 120 days from the start of the contract. The prototypes were produced in even less time, which everyone knew was a remarkable achievement. They had yet to realise just how remarkable.

In 1942, an RAF No 268 Squadron Mustang became the first RAF single-engine fighter aircraft to penetrate German airspace providing air support to a raid on the Dortmund. There followed further probing sorties, pushing their luck to see what was possible. This squadron also established some permanence of the type, retaining these aircraft until 1945. It redeployed to RAF Odiham north of Portsmouth some months later and used the experience gained to give the city, with its naval dockyards, and the south coast, some cover. They began intercepting intruder and reconnaissance missions, especially at early dawn and late dusk, when the Luftwaffe was most likely to mount them. From late 1943 onwards the whole squadron de-camped to RAF Turnhouse near Edinburgh to commence training to support large amphibious landings in the embarkment, transit and beach assault stages, but more particularly to exploit the Mustang's increasingly impressive fuel endurance which enabled it to loiter over target areas for lengthy periods of time. This was specifically targeted operational training for what would eventually be named Operation Overlord, the invasion and liberation of Europe from the west by American, British and Canadian forces. That it was coming was not in doubt on either side in the war, but the critical decisions about precisely where and when had to be kept a secret from both sides. As all the options were still under evaluation it was a guessing game anyway, but it did not stop a lot of people placing bets, including General Bernard Montgomery, who made a joke of it. It was suspected he might have benefited from inside information. Perish the thought.

Luftwaffe Intelligence had second-guessed something else. In the run-up to an invasion of Europe there would be strenuous attempts to disrupt strategic industrial assets such as U-boat production, oil production, transport infrastructure and aircraft construction. When the Casablanca Directive was signed by the Allied powers in early 1943, the destruction of aircraft production facilities within Germany was second on the list of priorities. There was only one way to do this. An onslaught of strategic bombing by the USAAF and the RAF based in England. The Luftwaffe had constructed a radar network covering western Europe that was operating as early as the middle of 1942. Increase in activity was noted. An air battle group comprising squadrons of Me 109s was moved west – 160 fighter aircraft. Moreover, the brand-new and formidable Focke-Wolf 190s were moved west too, as fast as they could be produced. The RAF was dismayed. They believed that the Mk 5 Spitfire was as good as it gets. It was not.

Rolls-Royce and Supermarine had to do better – they were the leaders in this arms race with Nazi Germany. They produced the Mk 9 Spitfire with two stages of supercharging combined with another single stage of turbocharging. Among other improvements this delivered almost another 10,000ft of fighting altitude. RAF Mk 9 Spitfire pilots took on Focke-Wulf 190s on a more than an equal basis.

The development of the Mustang started to become dispersed with different units authorised to try out different modifications. The biggest was the choice of whether to fit the Allison or the

Merlin engine as standard but with time and extension of role the choice of the Merlin became settled. Throughout the war the marque benefited from the ever-increasing power as Rolls-Royce continued to boost its power output. The RAF's complaints about restricted visibility were to a great degree solved by the replacement of rear-enclosed cockpit canopies with 'Malcolm' canopies. Named after their designer these improved visibility by raising the seat and fitting a clear frameless canopy. It was not beyond improvement however, and later it was NAA that came up with the best result by producing the 360-degree 'teardrop'. The top of the fuselage rear of the canopy was removed to complete the 360-degree vista. This reduced stability in yaw but was remedied by adding a dorsal fin. These modifications put the decisive finishing touch to the iconic image of the Mustang, no longer a bit of an ugly duckling, but sleek and showy.

Armament played a vital part. The machine gun with cannon mix could be varied according to role, and one marque – designated 1A – went the whole way and was armed with just the four 20mm cannon. It proved, unsurprisingly, very effective. No 168 Squadron was one example. Operating from the south of England these aircraft were deployed to roam over western Europe without any specific targeting orders. Codenamed 'Rangers', they were tasked to fly out over the Channel, search for targets of opportunity and destroy them. Externally carried bombs and rocket projectiles (RPs) became an option. 'Rhubarb' sorties were similar, but these focussed on finding and destroying designated targets. However, with the increasing range of the

Mustang, the pilots were often free to seek targets of opportunity on the recovery to base, and to attack them as well. In the armed reconnaissance role, the Allison Mustang was at its most impressive. One operation in particular, designated 'Poplar', was required to be executed only in poor weather – full-cloud cover with a base below 2,000ft. These were carried out by a sector pair of aircraft, in such weather conditions obviously adopting a low-level profile. The lead aircraft, on identifying the given target, called the run and turned his camera on. The wingman would break upwards to watch out for enemy aircraft circling just underneath the cloud base, while his leader concentrated on getting the photographs. Navigating at low level at 300 mph required concentration to find a pinpoint target while keeping clear of both ground obstacles and the lowering cloud. Should the pair be unlucky enough to encounter an enemy fighter the choices would include independently pulling up into the cloud, and returning to base separately, or staying low to try to fight off the opposition in a coordinated pair attack. The latter option would be fraught so close to the ground with so little in the way of the vertical dimension in which to manoeuvre. The standing instruction was not to seek engagement with enemy fighters but to use cloud to evade and escape. It seems to have been respected because in the admittedly short life of ACC only one Mustang was lost to an enemy fighter.

The Mustang began to roam further. It was deployed into North Africa to provide reconnaissance for interdiction of Axis supply lines. It provided tactical patrols to locate shipping in the

North Sea. Codenamed 'Lagoons', these sorties were primarily to locate enemy ships and to call in Coastal Command aircraft such as Mosquitos and Beaufighters to deliver the attacks. They were, in effect, acting as airborne forward air controllers.

During a mixed attack on the Pescara Dam in Italy in spring 1944, Mustangs assumed fighter-bomber mode and helped deliver a bomb-load sufficient to breach the dam.

RAF reconnaissance Mosquitos discovered some strange-looking apparatus in northern France. They looked like large bombs or torpedoes. Reconnaissance equipped Mustangs provided urgently needed close photography and the photographic interpreters were able to identify them as what turned out to be V-1 launch sites.

On D-Day, Mustangs were back into artillery spotting for naval units bombarding enemy positions in the immediate hinterland of the beachheads. Prompted by the D-Day landings the Germans began launching V-1 flying bombs at London. The V-1 was the first of Hitler's V (Vengeance) weapons, which sought to use the very latest scientific research and development to produce new innovative hi-technology weaponry. It was the first form of cruise missile. It comprised a torpedo-like casing, half of which was filled with fuel and half with high explosive. On top of the casing was mounted a pulse jet. A pulse jet burned fuel in a combustion chamber enclosed at the rear by a steel bulkhead containing a set of highly sprung steel vents. The fuel/air mixture was ignited by electric spark plugs and the increase in pressure caused by the ignited gases caused the vents to open and close against the spring pressure, releasing pulses of hot gas and flame to exit via the end of the jet pipe. This produced thrust and, assisted by a catapult, propelled the whole contraption up a ramp. Stub wings mounted on the sides developed lift to enable the V-1 to fly. It had automatic barometric control of its cruise altitude and was gyro-stabilized to prevent it from wandering off its computed heading and keep it flying straight and level. Some were partially guided, but all were aimed from close to the target, which needed to be large. London was large and the French coast was close, so many of the launch sites were along the Pas de Calais coast. The V-1 missile's fuel system was controlled by an air driven odometer that would shut it off at a time from launch when it was calculated it would be over London. The opening and shutting of the spring-loaded exhaust valves up to twenty times per second caused a very loud buzzing sound so these missiles were nick-named 'Buzz bombs'. Its threat and arrival was terrifyingly audible to the thousands of civilians who, not knowing its exact point of impact, had to take whatever cover they could. They knew they were all right if they could hear the engine. The sound would grow as it approached and if it started to fade those below knew it had passed them by. But if it stopped before that fade in volume, they could be at the trajected point of impact. Then, a few seconds later, came the explosion. Nearly 9,500 of these missiles were launched at London, around 100 a day when the campaign was at its peak.

The defence authorities had to work out a mix of countermeasures that included both ground anti-aircraft artillery and fighter aircraft. This combined effort they code-named 'Operation Diver'. There were several fighter aircraft types involved in these interceptions including Mosquitos, Spitfires, Tempests and the new twin-jet Gloster Meteor fighters. The Mustangs of No 133 (Polish) Wing were part of the air defence effort. The crew were placed at cockpit or crew room standby, and when an incoming raid was detected visually or by radar they were required to scramble, climb to the V-1s' observed altitude, anywhere between 2,000 and 9,000ft, and pick them up visually. On contact the fighter would turn into a six o'clock attacking position.

While it was all done in a hell of a rush, in one sense this was relatively simple combat because your 'adversary' was flying straight and level and could never do anything so unhelpful as throwing itself around in violent evasive turns. If your interception turn was good, there it sat in your gunsight, twelve o'clock, no deflection to worry about, large as life. There was just one other thing you had to get right though – the range at which you opened fire, always with cannon firing explosive shells, not machine guns, because machine gun bullets just bounced off its sheet steel fuselage. Only too easy in all the excitement to come barrelling in too close and forget you were about to open fire at a very large bomb. If you did, the blast could take your fighter down and you with it. A point worth bearing in mind.

The Mustang pilots were successful, coming third in the overall tally. Top scorers were Mosquitos destroying 625, Spitfires destroying 303, and Mustangs destroying 232.

In its introductory phase Allison-engine Mustangs had also developed an appetite for blowing up railway locomotives and the large barges that plied up and down the great rivers and canals of Europe, something like 400 in total. Although told not to seek engagement with enemy fighters, this was not always possible, and Mustang crews claimed about thirty fighters shot down as their range allowed them to fly 'Rangers' further and further out into enemy-occupied Europe.

Notwithstanding, General Brooke's fierce opposition did bring about the disbandment of the Command at the beginning of 1943, but the RAF was quietly ready for that possibility. At the point of disbandment, the units of the ACC were simply transferred to a new, bigger formation called the Second Tactical Air Force (2 TAF), whose function – combined integrated air-army-navy operations – was the same and more. Operation Overlord would be well served.

Chapter 3

Strategic Bombing

The rate increased at which brand-new bombers, especially the B-17 Flying Fortresses and the B-24 Liberators were being pushed out of the Boeing factory in Seattle, Washington, and the Consolidated factory in San Diego, California. The US Eighth Army Air Force 8thAAF (as it was renamed) began to deploy to hastily prepared bases in south-east England. There were further conversations between the British and the Americans about tactics. The British continued to insist, based on their shocking experiences early in the war, that daylight attacks were not the way to victory because of the vulnerability of big, heavy, overloaded bombers to fast, nimble, fighter aircraft armed with rapid forward-firing guns. Their acceptance of Duhet's vision of the invulnerability of big formations of heavy bombers by virtue of numbers, speed and protective firepower had evaporated. They believed that bombers unescorted by fighters needed the cover of darkness to reduce their losses to sustainable levels.

US strategic thinking, however, had not so changed. Their confidence was that with the B-17 and the B-24 the US 8thAAF would have at its disposal two state-of-the-art bombers which, flying huge tight formation boxes of aircraft bristling with machine guns, could beat the odds that had been encountered by the RAF. They believed that they could make such tactics prevail in daylight.

The British had not only changed to attacking at night, they had put in place programmes to switch from medium to heavy bombers and did so with urgency. Short Brothers of Belfast were awarded the first contract for a four-engine heavy machine, which they named the Sterling. The second contract awarded was to Handley Page of Radlett in Hertfordshire. With an eye clearly on outperforming the Sterling, they produced the Halifax. Lastly and best, A.V. Roe of Manchester produced the Lancaster. The night part of the strategic air offensive had already commenced.

United States defence procurement thinking, having come to the same conclusion about four engines, eliminated competing contenders and concentrated on the Boeing B-17 Fortress and the Consolidated B-24 Liberator. Unfortunately, in the foregoing development phase during the late 1930s, the B-17 had not performed brilliantly in some of the proving competitions with tragedy accompanying it. One prototype crashed on take-off due to failure to remove the control locks, killing the test pilot and destroying the aircraft. This, however, was caused by human error and not a design fault, so the testing and development went on. The trials and the development programmes continued, supported by a loyal following inspired by what might be possible when these setbacks were eradicated.

Their persistence was rewarded and eventually bombers went into production.

Of the threats to their bombers, the high commands of both countries were concerned with flak. 'Flak', an abbreviation of *'Fliegerabwehrkanone'*, (anti-aircraft cannon) included the fearsomely effective Krupps 88mm cannon. Albert Speer, responsible for the economic production of the Reich, revealed after the war that the RAF and later the USAAF had contributed to the war on the eastern front in a way that might not have been so obvious at the time. The Krupps 88 had been designed and intended primarily as an anti-tank weapon, and as an anti-aircraft gun only secondarily. Notwithstanding, thousands of them had to be withdrawn from the Russian war to defend German cities against Allied air attack, which helped swing the balance on the eastern front in favour of Russian army tanks. These guns were ground-placed but highly mobile. The danger, it was thought, could be obviated by flying at high altitude or making constant changes of heading. To bring the former into play needed a decision to fly very high, which brought with it serious problems to be examined later. There were also limits as to what could be achieved with the latter because continual changes of heading would ruin the bombardier's aiming on a bombing run. The bombing runs were lengthy and required a period of straight and level flight to acquire a target. Flak was nerve-wracking in its persistence but at high altitude was the lesser of two evils. The great threat came from the fighters.

The USAAF continued to refine their big formation, heavily-armed doctrine. Scores of aircraft would form up into a series of tight 'boxes' within which the bomber pilots flew close formation in pre-briefed patterns. These patterns looked level when seen in plan form from above or below, but the aircraft were staggered at different altitudes to confuse the height calculations of the flak-gunners. The B-17 boasted armour, not a significant amount when considered against the fearsome firepower they faced, but which, nevertheless, degraded their bomb-load capability. Their main answer was that the Fortresses were equipped with no less than thirteen machine guns each. A box containing thirty Fortresses would bristle with nearly 400 guns. Some were in the top of the fuselage (dorsal turrets) to provide mutual cover from above. Some were at the waist of the aircraft to fend off attack from the side. Some gunners were cramped into ventral cupolas slung underneath the aircraft with their knees up to their chest and nothing but the earth 12 miles below them. Below the tail fin was the rear-facing rear gunner who observed things in a parallel world where everything he saw had just happened. It was reckoned that a formation of thirty so-armed aircraft was capable of blasting out about a third of a million rounds a minute and that could stop anything. Impressive maths, but the maths didn't work as envisaged because a single Fw190 didn't expose itself to the whole group, but just a small bit of it. They also didn't work because an attacking fighter was in and out of shot within a very few seconds. Most of all they didn't work because the Luftwaffe pilots were quick to see that there was no significant forward firing capability with these bombers – they had an Achilles' nose. So, unsurprisingly, Luftwaffe fighter pilots did what was unanticipated in the design of the B-17; they attacked head on. Aiming the fighter straight at the front of the bomber and with a closing speed of up to 700mph they hammered away until the last split second before pulling out. Even if a burst did not damage the bomber's structure badly it was concentrated on the front, on the pilot, the co-pilot, the navigator, and the bombardier. With one or two key crewmembers killed or maimed, the bomber was likely to be rendered *hors de combat* and in bad shape to break out of formation and survive the long trip westward. They would probably still be harried by fighters who could easily spot wounded beasts and, like a pack of wolves, dive in to finish them off. The high-speed head-on tactics with Me 109s sometimes firing rockets, denied the American air-gunners a possible target. After the first devastating pass the fighters would pull up and from high above the bombers, roll-turn, put the nose back down and scream in for another attack; and another. Shortly, ammunition exhausted, the Luftwaffe pilots dropped out of the battle and set heading for base to refuel, rearm and wait for the next scramble order to get airborne. They would be vectored up once again for a second deadly bite, possibly at the same bomb group as they returned for home.

The addition of turbo-supercharging was a partial answer because it pushed up the B-17's service ceiling dramatically. The Me 109s could match those altitudes, especially when the bombers were outbound and carrying a heavy bomb load, but the thin atmosphere robbed the fighters of much manoeuvrability and speed margin. The RAF, keen to take the advantage that supercharging offered, proposed to use cruise altitudes around 30,000ft close to the top extremity of the Fortress' service ceiling for the protection from fighters this would afford.

The 'Forts' were neither pressurised nor heated. Thirty years after this time, the author flew unpressurised RAF jet aircraft at and above these altitudes. It demanded thorough training including experiencing the effects of high altitude in a decompression chamber and medicals to ensure the pilot was physically fit to cope with cockpit hypoxia, and other associated conditions. The orders associated with this flying were significant. Time flying above 30,000ft was to be limited to 15 minutes to be timed by stopwatch. Time flying above 35,000ft was to be limited to a strict maximum of 5 minutes. Such strictures give an indication of how close to the edge of human physical endurance B-17 crews fought. At least our cockpits were heated and quiet – the B-17s were not. Crews had to endure shattering levels of noise, the wretchedness of altitude sickness, and they regularly succumbed to frost bite in seriously sub-zero temperatures.

No 90 Squadron of RAF Bomber Command was the first squadron to receive Fortress 1s. Manning the squadron was slow because the special medicals to test fitness for high altitude conditions failed over 60 per cent of applicants, including previously experienced aircrew.

The aircraft didn't like extreme altitudes either. The Wright Cyclone engines might unload lubricant; the turbochargers became particularly petulant and occasionally blew apart. Other aircraft systems, not designed to cope with stresses incurred by the changes in temperature and pressure encountered in a climb from ground level to 30,000ft, developed insidious faults. Things could become dangerously unreliable until experience, analysis, and engineering modifications steadied things down. This took time.

When battle testing, further criticalities emerged. High altitude bombing accuracy depends on the quality of the bombsight equipment. The Norden bomb sight became famous, at least in part due to strenuous efforts by the US authorities to keep it a closely guarded secret. In early days this included installing it in an aircraft immediately before a mission and removing it immediately afterwards – all under armed guard and guaranteed to attract attention. In fact, the Norden sight was not the only game in town. There was another available made by Sperry of equal quality. Whatever the equipment, it required a clear view of the target from 20–30,000ft above it, depending on your attack profile. The device was tested and celebrated over the hot deserts of America. Being deserts, they were not famous for fog, rain, or overcast cloud. Europe was. This was a constant drawback. It also needed an ability positively to identify the target from several miles out, and to steer accurately and without significant disturbance towards it on the bombing run. This enabled the device to calculate the bomb release point and, under the gimlet stare of the bomb-aimer, to feed corrections to the autopilot to adjust the aircraft's track over the ground. It must have felt like an eternity to the aircrew who were now watching this great machine flying on automatic, unaided, lumbering inexorably towards its given target. To say nothing of all the scores of other Fortresses that were hanging on to each other's wing tips, the whole formation then hanging on to your aircraft if you happened to have the lead bomb-aimer as part of your crew. That was a lot of pressure.

The Americans and the British were, however, in complete agreement that strategic bombers had an absolute need to be heavily armed with defensive guns. There was less of a consensus about fuselage and wing armour, with the Americans favouring more protection for the crew while the British were reluctant because of the reduction in bombload that this would entail. It was possible to arrive at a broad consensus however, making possible the entrance of the B-17 flown by Royal Air Force crews. They had had named it the 'Fortress 1'and RAF Fortress 1 bombers were the first B-17s to enter combat against Germany. After several months, the results, prejudiced by the problems encountered, were not encouraging. The new high-altitude tactics proved no answer to vulnerability during daylight attacks while at the same time requiring a drastic reduction in bombload to get that high. And the climate over Europe took the sting out of the Norden bomb sight. What was there left to be tried next? Whatever it was, it was going to have to work.

Chapter 4

Tactical Superiority – Overlord

By July 1942, sixteen RAF squadrons had been re-armed with Mustangs. From the start, armed tactical reconnaissance became regular business. These Ranger missions were assigned specific targets to photograph, but also briefed to destroy any target of opportunity that presented itself. They flew in battle pairs. The land within a few miles of the coast along western Europe was covered regularly, as were the adjacent sea areas seeking out hostile vessels, these latter missions being code-named Lagoons. There were losses, some to enemy action, but worryingly, also to engine failures.

Raiding was an important and realistic preparation in the inventory of warfare. Preparation maybe, but it involves real fighting against an existential enemy. Historians of the Roman Army point out that along with techniques and tactics (the phalanx, the short sword, leading with the shield, formation drill that could change in an instant at the command of a Centurion's whistle) the main critical success factor in its long history was realistic training. It was a relentless daily requirement in peacetime. It was as hard as it could be made without actually chopping legionaries' limbs off. One commentary stated that training was battle without blood, and battle was training with blood. In modern warfare, raiding would fall into the latter category.

The Dieppe raid, code-named Operation Jubilee, was a trial in most of its respects – especially true because a doctrine contending with Douhet's thinking – integrated combined operations – was being tested for efficacy. It was to gain experience and rehearse integration of participating units – air, land, sea, command and control, intelligence, and flexibility in the fog of battle. It was also attrition to see whose side's destructive power was the greatest in a battle.

It comprised a force of mainly Canadian troops with the British Army in support. It was anticipated that this would be fiercely opposed by a Luftwaffe more experienced than Allied air power in integrated Wehrmacht/Luftwaffe combined operations. There would have been an awareness that, as the Germans had demonstrated time and again, they were good at this. Deployment using a wide set of integrated operational skills and equipment had been honed by a great deal of fighting during their four years of conquest in Europe. The raid was to test the Allies abilities to storm and capture an enemy occupied port. The strategic importance of capturing enemy occupied ports was that the Allies would need them as entry points for the main invasion of Europe.

Around sixty Allied squadrons were placed at readiness. They comprised a mix of all the top Allied fighter types. Hawker Hurricanes and Typhoons, Supermarine Spitfires and four squadrons of Mustangs made up this fighter force. The Mustangs were assigned their usual tactical low to medium level armed reconnaissance sorties, but this time there was a difference. Instead of taking off from east and southeast England, sweeping undetected over western Europe and wreaking havoc with relatively low risk of interception, this battle was pitched. Once the approach of the invasion was detected the Luftwaffe knew exactly where they had to go to engage. It was not a happy result. The Luftwaffe fought determinedly and shot down ninety RAF aircraft of which ten were Mustangs. This was aggravated by the fact that, during 1942, no fewer than a further forty Mustangs had been lost in training or other mishaps. It looked like the training was being over-pushed on a high-performance aircraft, which had to be flown with piloting skills that matched it.

The air battle itself would have both tactical and strategic import. Tactically, air superiority had to be achieved to protect Allied ground units from attack from Luftwaffe fighter-bombers. Strategically, air supremacy – defeat by shooting down a large number of Luftwaffe aircraft and killing or capturing the crews committed to this enormous battle – was to stretch the effectiveness of the Luftwaffe over the entire continent. By implication therefore, a wholesale Luftwaffe response to the Dieppe raid was not only anticipated – it was hoped for. The raid had among its purposes to bring the Luftwaffe up into the most critical air battle for the Western Allies since the Battle of Britain.

The Luftwaffe was indeed brought to battle in force but in what had been intended as a showdown, the numbers went the Luftwaffe's way with the allies losing 120 of their participating warplanes. The RAF had been tasked to protect the troops on the beach heads and the 240 ships that had conveyed them hence and would return them to England on a planned withdrawal. They had deployed squadrons in the largest air operation in the war to date. The Luftwaffe planes were equal to anything the Allied air forces could put into the air and, in the hands of veterans tempered by four years of war, they inflicted grievous losses. The air battle was tactically a victory for the Luftwaffe – they shot down more aircraft than they lost. It was, however, a strategic success for the Allied air forces because the Luftwaffe lost air superiority and did not ever regain it in that region of Europe. Mauled and drastically reduced as they were, the withdrawal of Allied forces back to England was largely uninterrupted.

In the ground battle, Jubilee was a dress rehearsal for the Allied invasion from the west, the commencing action to the liberation of the whole of Europe from the Pas de Calais to Berlin. But, as the Canadians waded ashore, they had been met with a withering storm of machine gun fire from weapons that had already been zeroed-in along their positions in the sea walls. The attacking forces were devastated. Around 6,000 troops embarked in England – 5,000 Canadian soldiers, and 1,000 British. A mere 2,000 made it back to the point of departure in England the majority having been killed or captured. This was a catastrophe. It comprised the worst allied single day of losses of the Second World War so far. But they say that the lessons that need to be learned are more obvious in failure cases than in successes. By the merciless criteria of battle, Dieppe was valuable. The time gap between the initial air and naval bombardment and the infantry hitting the beachheads had been too long, allowing enemy defenders to catch their breath and re-brace. The arrival of armour was similarly tardy, frequently having bogged down. Instead of the planned, overwhelming effect of continuous waves of air, artillery, armour and infantry, there were unfortunate unplanned pauses. Wehrmacht soldiers were being challenged with an attack plan that was ill-executed and one they could cope with. There were to be more, but smaller, raids along the French North Atlantic coastline. These consolidated the lessons learned. The drive for improvement continued.

There were other raiding attempts to draw the Luftwaffe into a decisive battle, most notably, in late 1943, the intriguing Operation Starkey. The British remained desperate to fatally weaken the Luftwaffe or finally destroy it, a strategic necessity that was still far from being achieved. The RAF pilots were veterans and their confidence was increasing with experience. They had no doubt about the critical need to control the airspace over any potential battlefield before the fighting started in earnest. No more repeats of Dieppe.

Operation Starkey wished to portray itself as a very large invasion. It was no such thing, but it did have objectives. The first was more practice in putting together a large, combined operation and launching it to sea. Secondly, reinforcing the Germans' expectations of an invasion at the Pas de Calais focussing on an attack on Boulogne. Thirdly, as in Jubilee, to bring up the Luftwaffe to battle in large numbers; and of course, any naval units that the *Kriegsmarine* was instructed to commit. Fourthly, a huge rehearsal and reconnaissance that although mounted at the time as a feint, could have been changed in short order should events reveal that Boulogne was a better prospect than Normandy. This latter comprised a bit of second guessing, in that if the Germans concluded this was a feint, which it was, it might rapidly be changed into the real thing. However, there was opposition amongst Allied senior officers that it might be a bit too clever by half, and the resources allocated to the overall operation were drastically reduced making the possibility of a real invasion out of the question.

The United States and British air forces commenced with bombing infrastructure. This was widened to include tactical targets such as fuel dumps and airfields. Over 800 warplanes were involved in an operation which culminated in a concentration on heavy coastal gun-batteries to confirm minds that a seaborne invasion was imminent. The armada of 350 ships sailed on 9 September escorted by Royal Navy destroyers, but the ships were completely empty of troops! What had begun as a feint now really was a charade. How much the Germans had got to know about the truth is not known but, in the event, they did not over-react, and at mid-morning the huge naval columns turned in glorious but ineffectual unison and returned to their ports.

The North African Campaign provided further opportunity to rehearse. Mustang squadrons not selected to participate in Jubilee were assigned to a broad programme, similarly practising and developing aspects of combined operations. Experience was gained raiding in Africa and Italy. North Africa became a theatre campaign in its own right. It was the opening show between two proud, hardened armies. The recently appointed General Bernard Law Montgomery briefed his troops that there would be no more withdrawals; that he had ordered all plans for withdrawal were to be destroyed – and at once. He said there had been much talk about Rommel but implied he was over-rated and said it would be quite easy – they were going to hit him a crack and have done with it.

'Monty' was a man of unshakable confidence. His command of his division covering the withdrawal at Dunkirk had brought admiration and gained him rapid promotion. Disturbed by what he had witnessed in the trenches during the First World War he was careful with his soldiers' lives – and they knew it. However fierce he was over policy and strategy with his high-ranking contemporaries, he showed consideration to his soldiers, who fought hard for him. He was not an easy man to get on with and his self-assuredness made him enemies unnecessarily. He was, however, undoubtedly a master of planning and preparation and despite being urged on by the grandees, would insist on holding back an advance until reserves, equipping and training were fully in place and ready. Winston Churchill said of him,

> 'Indomitable in retreat, invincible in advance, insufferable in victory.'

General Eisenhower, the Supreme Commander, had the wisdom to appoint as his deputy the RAF senior officer commanding his air forces, and who had what Kipling called 'the common touch'. Air Marshal Arthur Tedder was subtle and persuasive, skilled at winning over what later became known as 'hearts and minds.' This appointment surprised many, but Eisenhower said that he know of no one better at persuading others to his point of view than Tedder. Trust and influencing through persuasion was his style. *The Times* said of him,

> '... the most unstuffy of great commanders, who could be found sitting cross-legged, jacketless, pipe smouldering, answering questions on a desert airstrip.'

Tedder was a clear-thinking intellectual. He knew that concentration of force was the prime principle of achieving victory in any battle – land, sea or air. Eisenhower too was of the strong conviction that force concentration was a force multiplier, and that aircraft were not just a tactical innovation such as tanks, however game-changing tanks had become. The battlefield contribution of aircraft was essential to the movements of armies.

To give air cover from disruption by enemy fighter-bombers. To punch holes in enemy displacements allowing the advance of armour and ground-holding infantry. To deploy paratroops to interdict enemy supply lines and cut off reinforcements before they could be deployed.

As ground attack and armed reconnaissance aircraft, Mustangs had to deal with withering enemy flak – including some from Allied guns, which were hitting their own aircraft. It was from such tragedies that the decision was taken to reverse the work done to camouflage aircraft. Against a generally dark background, Allied tactical aircraft were made deliberately conspicuous and unmistakably different from Luftwaffe machines. They were painted with broad white stripes above and below the inner chords of their wings as well as vertically across their fuselages behind the cockpit. This was especially urgent for Mustangs. Allied fighters and fighter-bombers of a similar size such as the Hurricane and Typhoon had rounded wingtips. The Spitfire's wings curved forward into an elliptical point. The Mustang, by contrast, was given squared wingtips for ease and economy of manufacture. These made the Mustang look like, and all too easily be mistaken for, a Messerschmitt 109. The stripes made a big contribution to solving the problem. They found themselves increasingly operating together with Hurricane squadrons. The Mustangs could be armed with ground attack weapons while the 'Hurries' flew top cover to protect them from attack by enemy fighters.

Back in Europe, more Mustang squadrons found themselves running exercises without access to the comforts of their station messes. They were deployed to enjoy the pleasures of the outdoors in tents. Appropriately called Operation Spartan, this was literally a down-to-earth introduction to life as it was expected to be when sufficient progress had been made after the Overlord landings to warrant the establishment of temporary airfields on continental Europe. The news broke that RAF Army Cooperation Command was to be disbanded and replaced, and as already described, this seemed to be because of differences at the top over tactical doctrine. In its place there was to be a 'Tactical Air Force' (TAF) including British and American units. Those at the top of this new organisation took as their exemplar the North African campaign where the establishment of combined operations, especially under the persuasive guidance of Air Marshal Tedder, had made this work well for the embattled troops. The entire air effort for Overlord was not to be regarded, nor to operate, as a discrete air element as it undoubtedly was during the Battle of Britain. It was to be the air fighting arm protecting the sea passage to the landings and the embattled armies on the ground.

For the Mustang units the critical reconnaissance demands never abated. Pairs of Mustangs were dispatched to photograph artillery batteries in particular. It was deemed of vital importance to achieve complete mapping of the entire conflict area. Mustangs were ideally suited to carry out these sorties and did so along with Spitfires and Mosquitos. Mustang squadrons of the RAF and the United States Army Air Force continued flying a mix of operational sorties and preparatory training sorties. They did not know the go date of Overlord of 6 June 1944, so they maintained momentum by attacking false targets in Hampshire and Suffolk. As with Roman legionaries, this was battle without blood.

Training with blood came shortly afterwards, testing tactics in skirmishes. Patrols flown at low level to increase surprise and make the aircraft more difficult to hit from ground batteries could produce contacts with the enemy without much warning, so pilots had to be on their mettle. It was safer not to fly as a singleton. The Luftwaffe would operate in a loose formation of four aircraft known as a *schwarm* (swarm), or sometimes as a pair. In one encounter, two Mustangs were out on 'a sweep' when, unusually, they were bounced by a single Me 109. Taken by surprise they spotted the 109 dropping onto them like a stone and by agreement on the radio broke into hard turns in opposite directions and then into a spiral defensive dive. The 109 pilot chose to attack the wingman who pulled hard on the turn to a point where he was just beginning to 'grey-out' (lose visual acuity due to g-forces). The wingman was now acting as a lure while his leader manoeuvred into an attacking position. The German pilot seemed experienced and countered this. His initial move had been to use his height and speed in the dive to level the odds by taking out one of the pair in the first pass; then using the dive speed to pull up again hard to recover the height advantage for an attack on the second Mustang on a one-on-

one basis. It was a courageous tactic – he was on his own – but once it had failed the better part of valour would have been to use that speed to disengage completely and into cloud. He chose not to do so. He dived right down to tree-top level and tried to continue the fight. Having not reduced the odds to two fighters of equal performance and having lost the advantage of height and speed, he was shot down.

Overlord opened with an air assault by 23,000 paratroopers in order to have tactical support in position before the main forces came ashore. For the RAF's Mustang squadrons, the preparatory sorties continued right up to the go date of 6 June, and during the go date itself. Then, still without pause, the attacks went on beyond the difficult and costly breakouts from the beach heads, into the push east. There could be no let up now. As with Roman Legionaries, hard training had run seamlessly into battle fighting. Initially, there was heavy emphasis on low level defensive protection of surface units by Mustangs, Hurricanes and Tempests, with Spitfires and Thunderbolts layered above at higher altitudes to take on Luftwaffe fighters. It brought an important success. Air superiority was wrested from the Luftwaffe over a long strip along the Normandy littoral making it possible to advance to the east.

The struggle to break out of the beachheads went better in some places than others. Beachheads were extremely dangerous places. They were obvious killing zones. It was unmistakable where they were, that attacking troops had to transverse them at some point, at which time they would be concentrated and vulnerable. The Axis engineers had enjoyed ample time to prepare well. They had built modern fortifications referred to as the 'Atlantic Wall'. It was a wide strip of lethal and diverse defensive measures, which incorporated natural features such as rivers rather than an actual wall. It was ingeniously and formidably constructed. Manned by over 100,000 German troops, it was furnished with artillery of all sizes. The German Army, as in the First World War, had the critical advantage of being strategically on the offensive but tactically on the defensive. On Omaha beach, where the naval and air bombardments had been less successful than hoped in destroying enemy coastal defences, disaster was only narrowly avoided.

The German defences were not all static under concrete gun emplacements. It was known that an SS Panzer (Armoured) Division was stationed to the north. Breakout momentum had to be gained before these units could move or once again the result would be in doubt along with mass casualties. Some of the many feints and deceptions that the Allied forces had carried out were highly successful. These included an army of life-sized dummy rubber tanks, planes and transport vehicles based opposite the Pas de Calais, all easy to detect by Luftwaffe reconnaissance planes (Operation Fortitude). Additionally, they let it be discovered by German Intelligence that this 'army' had been placed under the command of the American General George Patton. Patton was regarded by Wehrmacht high command as the best American fighting General, and this made the ploy even more convincing. They, (including Hitler, a compulsive meddler in strategic matters) remained convinced that the real attack would still come at Calais and held back the S.S.

Of the 130,000 troops that landed on 6 June, there were over 10,000 casualties. Grim as this was, in terms of proportionality it was nowhere near as grim as Jubilee had proved. But Jubilee had demonstrated that attempting to storm an occupied, fortified port was an option to be avoided if at all possible. Overlord concentrated on open beaches, and it proved the right choice. As the breakouts gathered momentum, vast numbers of reinforcements were able to pour ashore and in the next three weeks, 850,000 troops, along with huge quantities of fighting and support vehicles and thousands of tons of stores and equipment were landed to be thrown into the fray. There was cutting edge technology such as the new Mulberry floating harbours. PLUTO (Pipeline Under the Ocean) enabled fuel to be pumped ashore without interdiction of oil tankers by U-boats, aircraft or mines. The Decca navigation system was developed for use by the Royal Navy to clear mines prior to assaulting the beach heads, a system that was used world-wide by ships and aircraft until it was closed down in the year 2000 when GPS was made available for public use. Seven thousand naval vessels from battleships right down to assault craft delivered the seaborne operations. These vessels not only carried the troops and swept the sea passages for mines, they guarded against U-boat, E-boat and air attack, and carried out naval bombardments of shore installations especially gun-batteries.

As the invasion troops began to break out and link up to push east, emphasis in the air support requirements changed. Ground reconnaissance was always in demand, therefore so were the Mustang squadrons. Ground attack using fighter-bomber Mustangs, became a priority. The need for big resources in air-to-air fighting slowly diminished as air superiority was wrested from the Luftwaffe by the Allied air forces, but patrolling continued at higher levels carried out mainly by Spitfires and Thunderbolts.

Nevertheless, fighter-bombers must be able to take care of themselves when necessary. To go from thinking bomber to thinking fighter is a challenge as the skill sets differ. And air fighting could be a very strange experience. Pilots regularly reported that one minute an air battle could be at a terrific crescendo, full of wheeling aircraft and tracer shells; but a few moments later they could find themselves in a completely empty sky. It reflected the speeds being achieved at combat throttle settings. Things happened very quickly. A Me 109 pilot, separated from his number two, spotted two Mustangs below him. He pushed forward the stick to bunt the plane into a dive. He could do this without his engine stopping or having to roll on his back to pull through because his engine was fuel injected. The Mustangs, in level flight, were quickly overhauled by the diving 109 and grew in his windscreen. He opened fire on the wingman, who didn't have a chance. The cannon fire badly damaged his Mustang but mercifully did not harm him. In a state of shock, the pilot pulled the canopy back, rolled the aircraft upside down and released the buckle. He fell clear of the cockpit and, at a rapid anxious count of three, pulled the D-Ring on his parachute. There was a jerk as his canopy deployed that made him gasp. All the roaring and windblast suddenly ceased and he found himself floating down, aware only of a whispering wind.

The leader of the pair pulled around hard to the point that his vision started to grey out. He eased back on the stick to get his sight back, and there it was, still dodging and weaving, the Me 109. The Luftwaffe pilot must have lost sight of the Mustang behind him. The American opened fire. There was an explosion far in front. The Luftwaffe pilot pulled hard away into a right-hand turn but the aircraft went into a dive trailing smoke. The pilot bailed out. The lead American pilot then spotted another Me 109 above him. The enemy was high, and that was a bad position for the Mustang. He pulled up to bring his guns to bear. But the 109 pilot seemed to be in a dream. He was not weaving. Picking up the flashes past his wings half a second too late and not appreciating his adversary was below him, he tried to push out of it and dropped straight through the Mustang's gunsight and a blast of bullets. The sky was now empty – everything had vanished! Critical on fuel he turned the Mustang north-west for home. His wingman landed in a field and broke an ankle. Unable to evade he was quickly captured and spent some months in a prison camp until it was eventually overrun by advancing American troops.

Ground attack remained a vital priority, so the Mustang was given plenty of opportunity to shine. It was proving to be a formidable single-engine, fighter-bomber able to carry two 500lb bombs from release points under its wings. Air to ground rocket projectiles were also an option. On internal fuel only it still retained an impressive loiter time over the battle area. Trials were carried out with an additional centre-line external fuel tank, which could be jettisoned prior to an attack. The Allison engine Mustang was, of course, originally designed for this work, and it did not disappoint. Such attacks might be both for designated targets or for targets of opportunity. The fighter-bombers, Mustangs and Mosquitos, would race in at low level, with Thunderbolts, Hurricanes and Spitfires flying top cover above to prevent enemy fighter interference. This was largely successful. Even so, attacking ground targets within a battle area bristling with anti-aircraft guns remained unsuitable for those of a nervous disposition. That was not going to change any time soon. The work went on.

Chapter 5

Strategy and Politics

The Royal Air Force was shaped between the wars primarily as a bomber force. There was an increasing adherence to the writings of Giulio Douhet, the Italian strategy theorist, which included British Prime Minister Stanley Baldwin. Baldwin, who dominated British politics between the two world wars, stated to The House of Commons in 1932,

'The bomber will always get through.'

Translated into policy, this implied that countries should arm themselves with bomber fleets capable of inflicting unacceptable damage on an enemy. It sounded aggressive, but sounding aggressive can be a form of peace-making. It was the age-old strategy of deterrence.

The optimum outcome, the safest and cheapest situation, would have been an international ban on bombers. But the international system, faced for the second time in little over thirty years with deliberately belligerent potential enemies, critically lacked trust. British Prime Minister Neville Chamberlain's 'piece of paper' guaranteeing that Britain and Germany would never go to war with one other again made no impact. To do that you had to be convinced that the parties to a treaty or an assumption, were good for the promise. If you were not, you had to continue to arm yourself because you could never be sure that the other side would not steal advantage by arming anyway. When Game Theory – the mathematical science of strategy – emerged, it encapsulated this in a scenario called the Prisoner's Dilemma. The optimum solution, based on trust, failed for the lack of it. Everyone armed. However, strategic stability was established by the mutually shared notion that any attack on another state would inevitably bring disastrous retaliation upon the aggressor. This is multiplied if states enter treaties that will enforce that principle to the benefit of the signatories. The stability conferred by the North Atlantic Treaty Organization (NATO) is the most successful example of this since the decline of the British Empire. Article 5 of the treaty states that an attack on one of its members shall be mutually deemed an attack on them all. So, there would be peace, albeit an uneasy one.

In the 1930s, the thinking about achieving a stable balance based on mutually assured retaliation changed. There emerged a realisation that strategic advantage might be gained by producing fleets of fast, nimble fighter aircraft, capable of shooting down bombers before they struck. One's own cities might be protected from destruction by such fighter planes. In a process game theorists first came to call 'escalation', all protagonists had to have both tactically-defensive fighters and strategically-offensive bomber fleets to balance and re-stabilise the strategic equation.

What sort of a bomber fleet should a nation have? Here there was a difference in thinking between Britain and Germany. Germany opted for large fleets of medium bombers – twin engine machines such as the Junkers 88 and the Dornier 217. Britain, having tried medium bombers and finding them ineffective, came to believe the future was with heavy bombers and went all out for four-engine types – the Short Sterling, the Handley Page Halifax, and the Avro Lancaster.

The Battle of Britain in 1940 confirmed to the British that the total annihilation of populations by fleets of attacking bombers as argued by General Douhet and described graphically by H.G. Wells in his novel *Things to Come*, had not yet arrived. The Luftwaffe medium bombers simply could not match the manoeuvrability of single engine RAF Hurricanes and Spitfires and while some of them did get through it was at an unsustainable price in battle losses.

In the years running up to the Second World War there was urgent concentration on bomber development. The United States was not, however, concerned with aggressive strategic campaigns, but with the defence of the nation's long coastlines. The USA assumed that its neighbours, Canada and Mexico, were not potential threats. As for the rest of the world, there was no aircraft type that could fly in from the east, the North Atlantic, without the probability of being detected in plenty of time and certainly not achieve a round trip from continental Europe with a significant bomb-load. From the North Pacific, dwarfing even the North Atlantic, the distances were substantially greater. Any coastal threat would therefore be delivered from an enemy fleet capable of mounting long range operations, and that could mean aircraft carriers with light bombers, surface raiders such as those being constructed by Germany, or a submarine threat to surface shipping. From the Pacific, California, Oregon and Washington states were deemed vulnerable, but also Hawaii and Alaska including the Aleutian Islands. There were also small, far-flung outlying islands that could have strategic importance. One of these was called Midway.

The east coast benefitted from the existence of the Intracoastal Waterway, comprising an inland route that linked natural rivers and estuaries with large man-made canals stretching from Texas to Massachusetts. This obviated need for much coastal merchant marine traffic, but U-boats could still prey on vessels attempting to cross the North Atlantic; and the coast might still come under naval bombardment. The German *Kriegsmarine* wished to use carrier-borne aircraft in the Second World War, but their building programmes were never brought to operational fruition. The Japanese however, had been deeply impressed by the Royal Navy's brilliant success when it sank the Italian fleet at the Battle of Taranto using only obsolescent carrier-borne torpedo bombers. They pressed on with their carrier building programme and completed it. Notwithstanding that outcome, strategic thinking is about possibilities, which must be watched with a view to countering them should they become existential threats.

An integral part of the defence of mainland USA was the proposal to develop a long-range bomber, able to challenge any hostile fleet before it got close enough to an American coast to be able to attack it. The traditional thinking in the US, as it had been in Europe, was for twin-engine machines. The four-engine option was slow to gain favour, but there was an inevitability about the four-engine proposal in that it could better meet the urgent need to match higher fuel loads with higher bomb loads to deliver them over greater ranges. A trade-off within the bomb-load-to-range ratio was no longer acceptable. There was no merit in achieving impressive ranges if this required reducing the bombload to levels inadequate for a decisive attack. By the same token, impressive bomb loads that could be carried only a short distance would not serve either. Four engines looked like a game changer.

The British had not had a good experience with twin-engine medium bombers, such the Bristol Blenheim and the Vickers Wellington, when they formed the spearhead of their attacks against the Reich. It became clear that by day they would be shot down by the Luftwaffe and flak guns in unsustainable numbers. They changed to night attacks, which reduced the loss rate, but the weight of bombs that such twin-engine machines could deliver remained insufficient to have any decisive effect. Moreover, in August 1941, the Butt Report, commissioned by Professor Lindeman, the scientific advisor and friend of

Winston Churchill, showed the accuracy of night bombing fell well short of both the unrealistic hopes of RAF senior officers and of enthusiastic aircrew guesses. The RAF had no means of assessing the effects of its bombing raids. Clearly the British needed a new start.

Throughout 1941, before America had even entered the war and President Roosevelt was still publicly adhering to a declared policy of international isolationism, he and Prime Minister Churchill had already agreed that in the event of another outbreak of general war the main protagonists would be Germany and Japan and that the defeat of Germany should be the first priority.

In the USA, the role and production of bomber aircraft remained continuously on the agenda. Decisions about suitable aircraft for strategic warplanes became centred around two contenders – the Boeing B-17 Fortress, and the Consolidated B-24 Liberator. The B-17 was favoured for the European theatre. Then, in December 1941, the Japanese Imperial Navy attacked Pearl Harbour in Hawaii. The United States declared war on Japan and her allies. For the United States there were now deadly enemies on the other side of both oceans – the Pacific and the Atlantic. The calculation of the numbers of heavy bombers required was so large that mass production of both types was essential to fight two separate wars. The Axis powers could not restrain themselves to believe that there might be more to be gained by caution than by unrestrained belligerence. To the east, the Nazis had conquered Europe in a shockingly brief time. To the west, the Japanese had seized an empire, also with breathtaking speed, against colony nations who were not trained, ready, or inclined to fight wars themselves. Their Imperial masters had performed abysmally and lost for the present. However, for the Japanese to see the United States as just a larger version of what their armed forces had encountered before December 1941 was a huge miscalculation. Of the Pearl Harbour attack, Admiral Yamamoto, who had spent considerable time in the United States and had overseen the attack himself, remarked gloomily that he feared Japan had aroused a sleeping giant and filled him with a terrible resolve.

The vastness of the Pacific narrowed enemy options from the west. To the east was a smaller ocean but which still put a prodigious distance between any potential European enemy and their coastline. The predictable scenarios remained – attacks by submarines or long-range surface vessels sinking commercial shipping; or naval fleets approaching a shoreline to bombard or launch tactical bombers from aircraft carriers. The island territories, at such distances from the US mainland, were particularly vulnerable. The war procurers continued the drive towards land-based, long-range heavy maritime bombers. These could react rapidly to any threat that had managed to approach American coastlines as soon as it was detected, including attacking it. So, the Boeing B-17 itself was originally designed as a long-range maritime patrol bomber.

First to form, the 2nd Bombardment Group became a crew test and development outfit, exploring and charting the flight envelope, establishing maximum speeds, fuel efficient cruising and altitude data; and thereafter calculating range and radius of action performance, climb to height times at different weights; and developing suggestions for tactics based on the data. It paid special attention to long-range navigation techniques and laid down proposals for standard procedures. Interception exercises were carried out on surface vessels at sea and were so successful that when news coverage unwrapped the story that a ship had been successfully intercepted over 700 miles from the Atlantic coast, this caught the sharp attention of the United States Navy. The Navy complained that the USAAC with these new long-range bombers was encroaching on their domain. To appease the Navy the 2nd Bombardment Group were instructed not to fly more than 100 miles from the coast, effectively clipping their wings as far as long-range operations (what they were designed for) were concerned. Moreover, the powerful Navy lobby persuaded Harry Woodring, the Secretary of State for War, to issue a directive instructing the USAAC to procure only tactical bombers just to make sure the point had been taken.

The Munich Crisis later in 1940 reversed all that wrong-headedness and, if there were any lingering doubts, the Japanese Imperial Navy rammed the point home at Pearl Harbour on the following year. This was the sort of siloed thinking that had hindered joint service operations on the other side of the Atlantic. There, in the light of hard experience and analysing what had given the Germans such an effective record of conquering, Allied thinking was changing. It was absorbing

P-51D with single centre-line external drop-tank. The external drop-tanks were made of feather-light reinforced papier-maché, and were critical in extending the fighter's radius of action and endurance.

Mustangs of 375th Fighter Squadron, 8th US Army Air Force, 1944. These aircraft have twin wing-mounted fuel drop-tanks.

An armorer loads .50 calibre ammunition belts into the Browning machine guns of a P-51B. Each belt was 27 feet long. A prolonged burst of fire that emptied the gun completely gave rise to the expression "Giving it the full nine yards."

Chuck Yeager's P-51D. Yeager scored 12 kills including two Me 262 swept-wing twin-engined fighter jets, the fastest warplanes of the Second World War. After the war Yeager became a test pilot and the first man to exceed the speed of sound.

Top scoring Mustang ace of the war, Major George Preddy shot down 23 enemy aircraft and destroyed five more on the ground by strafing. He was killed on Christmas Day 1944 at the age of 25, tragically by so-called "friendly fire".

Dramatic launch of a P-51. It looks distinctly carrier-like, but this was in fact at Iwo Jima.

A prototype B-17 Boeing Flying Fortress. It is bright silver, it's camouflaging yet to be applied.

Women technicians at work in the rear fuselage of a B-17, Long Beach, California.

Boeing B-17Fs showing the Bombardiers clear-view plexiglass nose.

Part of a large B-17F formation on one of the Schweinfurt ball-bearing raids over Germany, August 1943.

the realisation that 'smokestack' organisation, that is failure to achieve close cooperation between units whatever their service, would leave operational gaps for the enemy to exploit. It was not a doctrine that would deliver the all-important concentration and co-ordination of force.

Where strategic bombing was debated, many held significant reservations about targeting and avoiding the horrors of area bombing. They wished to hit industrial complexes without the angst of collateral damage to the surrounding residential areas. This ambition was consistent with an accuracy of bombing that could only be achieved in daylight. Not all were impressed by such conclusions. After two years of war losses, Air Chief Marshal Sir Arthur Harris, Air Officer Commanding Royal Air Force Bomber Command, had no sympathy with what he saw as unrealistic aspirations, however laudable. The matter was resolved by an agreement that while the RAF would continue to attack at night, the USAAC would attack during daylight hours, the combined arrangement giving no respite to the enemy from round the clock attacks.

And so it was that big differences of opinion, including moral differences, were eventually reconciled by, of all things, an arrangement between the two allied bomber forces to collaborate in round the clock bombing of Germany.

Chapter 6

On Regardless

At the same time as P51 Mustangs had started cutting their teeth in the tactical raiding world, the B-17 strategic bomber squadrons were arriving in the United Kingdom. After Herculean organizational, logistic, engineering and crew training efforts, the first tentative, experimental attacks were mounted over North Germany. These were abortive and inconclusive due to diverse factors, especially cloud and icing. There were also engine problems. To name one, the Wright Cyclone radial engines, turbo-supercharged to deliver 1,200hp had a habit of unloading lubricant especially in the climb. Such problems, eventually, were addressed, but there was little that could be done to get around bad weather.

In the beginning, fighters were rarely encountered at around 30,000ft due to the novelty of such high cruise altitudes. However, some got up there, but because Me109s were observed to have stalled while attempting attacking manoeuvres, it over-emphasized the extent to which altitude deteriorated the fighter's performance. This didn't last – the Luftwaffe also was learning how to cope.

Raids were tried at lower altitudes. Inevitably they were intercepted but again, initial results seemed encouraging. One

B-17 was intercepted by three 109s resulting in one fighter being shot down and the other two being damaged and driven off. The bomber sustained only minor damage. Instead of this incident being viewed critically as a possible lucky fluke, it was taken as a good sign confirming the 'bristling with machine-guns' argument – that aircraft so armed really could defend themselves. It was all to prove a false dawn, when a Fortress cruising above 30,000ft was attacked by a *schwarm* of 109s and sustained severe damage. The aircraft escaped via a long shallow dive into cloud but with crew injured and two dead. It managed the difficult recovery to base but caught fire on landing and was destroyed. Battle losses such as this increased as the Luftwaffe took a grip and developed tactics to deal with these new, high-flying intruders.

High altitude had drastically reduced the flak danger but had brought other problems with it. Higher altitudes reduced bomb-loads. Moreover, the Norden sight could not bomb a target that the bombardier could not see because of cloud, precipitation, smoke or darkness. The desire to target industrial sites accurately, while at the same time avoiding the horrors of collateral damage, was proving unachievable. This was the moral argument for daylight flying. Blind bombing technology and techniques had not been viewed necessary by the Americans and were not currently to their hand. These early raids were failures except they made shortcomings of machine and doctrine unavoidably clear. Misconceptions began to evaporate.

The RAF, on the other hand, had been developing blind bombing because it operated during the hours of darkness, so it was going to be available to all the Allied air forces as soon as the Americans came to see there was no practical alternative. What worked in darkness would work in cloud, smoke and rainstorms.

Fewer than fifty sorties had been flown when the force was stood down and dispersed. One flight was transferred to the North African theatre where desert conditions immediately began to degrade the aircraft. The wind was hot and contained fine sand particles, which abrased everything from wing leading edges to people's teeth. Eroded propellers lost thrust and the cooling fins on the great radial engines were reduced. Filters clogged almost as soon as they had been replaced and windshields became cloudy and translucent. High ambient temperatures further limited maximum take-off weights and, therefore, range and bomb-load. The situation was not viable. The bombers and the crews were withdrawn from the theatre.

The remaining part of the force had been assigned to RAF Coastal Command. In the role of long-range maritime patrol bomber, it met with some success at last. After all, it was the role for which the B-17 had been originally designed.

Whatever their doctrinal differences had been about day as opposed to night operations, both the Allied air forces knew it remained essential that their joint efforts had to be coordinated. The Allied armies were still reorganizing and working up. Their navies were flat out in a vast game of cat and mouse on the oceans, especially on the Atlantic where they were locked into the vital work of convoy protection. At that time the only effective way to bring the war to the enemy was to reduce Germany by strategic bombing. Abandoning the overall project was not an option.

A vast civil engineering project to build airfields commenced, the biggest by far ever undertaken in the United Kingdom. The British Air Ministry had long had a team of expert surveyors out looking for suitable sites for new airfields. They located many but in the end the largest number were earmarked for development in the countryside north of London and south of Leicestershire. These were allocated for use by the Bomb Groups.

Fighters, even heavyweights like the Republic P-47 Thunderbolt, didn't ask for much initially. If it was flat, smooth and well drained, they would happily take off and land on it. If your airfield was a commandeered former flying club, you had 'lucked in' as they said. They had toilets and everything. The bar may have been made of stacked crates, but you soon didn't care if it had bottles of beer in them. They didn't need much petrol relatively speaking, so a few replenished bowsers to hand would do it. Accommodation felt like sleeping in a garden shed (which may well have been the case), but there were bicycles with quaint wicker baskets on the front and a pub within cycling distance. The pub had draught beer and girls who quickly learned to jitterbug.

In the bomber world things could not have been more different. Heavy bombers required concrete runways, access peritracks, hard standings for parking, and a proper, three-storey control tower to manage air movements safely. Their bases needed hangars and workshops to accommodate 24-hour maintenance operations and huge storage capacity for equipment, fuel and thousands of aircraft spare parts, as well as everyday necessities like soap and shirts. Each base had to provide accommodation for over 2,000 personnel with electrical and water utilities. Flying began from each of these sites before the construction work had been completed. They retained a distinct building-site look for months. American servicemen posted to the inadequately drained Grafton Underwood in Northamptonshire sardonically referred to their new home as Grafton-Under-Mud.

But the combined civil engineering projects were astonishing by any standard. At Thorpe Abbots in Suffolk in England, the Laing company was allocated a flat area of 500 acres of farmland and contracted to build three runways with fifty bomber hardstands. The main east-west runway was a mile and a quarter long and the three runways were served by over 3 miles of peritrack. Eleven miles of concrete roads were built, 3 miles of sewers, 5 miles of water mains, 15 miles of storm drains. Three hundred buildings were constructed including two hangars and an air traffic control tower, all this using half a million square yards of concrete and 4 million bricks. There were sixty-seven such airfields constructed for the USAAF, largely in East Anglia. Unlike most of them, which have deteriorated into ghostly dereliction or been returned to agricultural use, Thorpe

Abbotts is still there and available to see as the 100th Bomb Group Memorial Museum.

The B-17 had a strong association with England. Boeing built over 12,500 of which 9,000 were assigned to operations flying from there; 8,300 were destroyed or written off as damaged beyond repair, many through accidents but mostly through enemy action. Of the crews, a mere 27 per cent survived their tour of twenty-five missions and the average number of missions completed by each crew-member was eight. These are grim figures. The USAAF cemetery at Madeley in Cambridgeshire, with its silence, clipped lawns and row after row of white headstones, will never be forgotten by anyone who has visited there to pay their respects.

Each US Bombardment Group (BG) comprised four squadrons established for ten bombers each. Operational flying had commenced in late summer of 1942 by the 97th BG. These were short range raids, comfortably within the radius of action of the supporting RAF Spitfires providing top cover. More BGs joined the fray including involvement in the Dieppe Raid (Operation Jubilee). Protected by RAF squadrons things looked set fair with little loss; and, for a while, a puzzling reluctance by the Luftwaffe to show up for work. The weather permitted visual bombing and infrastructure such as railway convergence points were urgent targets. In favourable summer weather, better results had been expected. They were disappointing and this lack did not portend well as the summer faded into autumn with its characteristic mists, early morning fog and low cloud cover.

In September the Luftwaffe struck back. They broke the pattern by arriving high above an attacking bomber formation and in force, raising questions afterwards about how they had achieved that. The Me 109s, with the advantage of speed, height, and surprise dived down through the fighter top cover and with alarming alacrity, destroyed two B-17s. And vanished. It was a nasty wake-up call.

As the weather worsened, bombing accuracy fell away. Success rates became poor. Flak guns had been re-deployed to concentrate on defending the most critical strategic targets from attack and became an increasing peril. High altitudes reduced the threat, but also the bomb-load carried, which implied more sorties to be flown, which implied more risk. There must have been an optimum there somewhere, but how this was calculated, if indeed it was, was not made clear to the aircrews taking those risks.

Arguments and revisions of tactics were continual. There emerged a reluctant acceptance that heavy aircraft in close formation, each controlling its own track and releasing their bomb-loads individually were running a very high risk of mid-air collision. On one occasion, two B17s collided with one bomber impossibly embedding itself on top of another. The top aircraft pilots shut down their four engines continuing to fly on the engines of the bottom plane over which, of course they had no control.

The connected pair of B-17s were flown using the controls of the top aircraft and crash landed in Germany. The landing impact freed the top aircraft which shot forward in one piece, but the bottom aircraft exploded into flame. The survivors were taken prisoner after what became known as 'the piggy-back flight'. The Germans imagined the Americans had introduced a new eight engine super-bomber. An extraordinary feat.

The high collision risk drove changes to standard operating procedures to reflect the thinking of General Curtiss LeMay. LeMay, a tough, rising officer, revered by his men who called him 'Old Iron Ass', set the pace for tactical development. He subsequently served a long career in bombers to become the Commanding Officer of Strategic Air Command, taking strategic bombing fully into the nuclear age. It is thought he was the inspiration for Brigadier General Jack Ripper in Stanley Kubrick's *Doctor Strangelove*. The bombardier in the lead aircraft would do the aiming for the entire formation. All the other aircraft would concentrate on accurate station-keeping within the formation. The bombardiers in the rest of the Group would release bombs when they saw the lead bombardier doing so from the lead plane. Collision risk was reduced but the technique had the disadvantage that there would be a time-lag between the release from the lead plane and the release from all the others, even supposing that all aircraft had a clear view of the lead plane. It was still a lot to ask of the crews. It was good enough for bigger targets but accuracy with smaller targets was not well served. This had been key to limiting collateral damage, the moral argument. Collateral damage gradually came to be seen as undesirable but unavoidable.

General Ira Eaker, the commanding General of the United States 8th Army Air Corps, and first to arrive in England, had to shoulder these problems. As the 8th Army Air Force attempted to prosecute the daylight strategic bombing campaign against Nazi-occupied Europe, things went badly. The strategy was right. The tactics employed, however, were flawed for lack of learning from others' experience about daylight operations, and the lack of strategic fighters to protect the bombers.

The RAF had originally subscribed to similar thinking. It was not just that their losses were terrible when they attempted day-light bombing – it was that they were mathematically unsustainable. So, they switched to night-time bombing. Flying the B-17, the US 8th Army Air Force senior officers remained confident that they could succeed where the RAF had not. Their tactical doctrine, that tight formations of bombers protected by armour-plating and heavy machine guns providing mutual cover throughout the formation, would be sufficient. Enough to ward off attacking Luftwaffe fighters, even in daylight. Notwithstanding that the RAF High Command might have been privately aghast; the arrangement did seem to comprise a powerful strategy. The RAF attacking by night and the USAAF by day meant that the Reich would have to endure the disruptions, the privations, the horrors and the casualties of round the clock bombing with no respite .

The B-17 itself was meant to be a tour de force but it was a mixture of good and not so good. It was faster than the RAF's best bomber, the Lancaster, by around 30mph and could climb to 30,000ft, which was not a practical prospect for the British-designed heavy bomber. However, there was a remarkable difference in bomb-load capability. On deep penetration missions, the B-17's bomb-load was typically 4,000lb and, in certain conditions, even less. The Lancasters, by contrast, were able to carry around three times the Fortresses' bombload. The disparity could be even wider with special weapons. The Tallboy 'earthquake' bomb weighed in at 12,000lb. This weapon destroyed the Saumur tunnel preventing reinforcement by German Panzers during the Dunkirk landings; and it sank the *Tirpitz* battleship proving that even such an enormous bomb could be delivered with surprising accuracy if you were lucky with the weather. After modification, the Lancaster was also able to lift and fly (just about) a staggering 22,000lb single Grand Slam – an even bigger earthquake bomb. Both those weapons were designed by Sir Barnes Wallace and were carried by No 617 Squadron, 'The Dam Busters'.

By British standards therefore, the B-17 was not a heavy bomber at all, but a medium bomber. Given the state of aircraft technology in the 1930s and 1940s, strengths were invariably achieved by compromising something else. One type of British medium bomber – the De Havilland Mosquito – demonstrated how these trade-offs could be made to work given a touch of radical ingenuity. Flying in the face of RAF doctrine – that all bomber aircraft must be armed with defensive guns – De Havilland knew that the heavy weight of those guns, with their turrets, hydraulics and ammunition, was at the expense of fuel load and consumption. This restricted the range of the aircraft, which in turn limited its ability to strike targets. It would be offensively compromised. It also limited altitude and speed performance, putting it within the very altitude/speed envelope where it would be vulnerable to fighter attack, so it would also be defensively compromised. It was a self-defeating result. But what if the guns, turrets and ammunition were removed? What if the plane was made of wood making it incredibly light? What if it was powered by two of the most advanced Rolls-Royce Merlin engines? Firstly, the range would increase to enable them to reach the furthest-flung targets. Secondly, the aircraft would have a power-to-weight ratio such that it could carry a significantly bigger bomb-load so high, so fast that it would be virtually invulnerable to flak and fighter interception – so the gunnery apparatus would not be needed anyway. This was a combination of trade-offs that worked beautifully.

In contrast, but in accordance with the same trade-off logic, protection in the form of armour and lots of defensive guns degraded the B-17's speed and altitude performance that put it dangerously back within the reach of flak and fighters – even with a severe sacrifice of bomb-load. This implied that to deliver the same tonnage as one Lancaster, the Fortresses had to make three round trips incurring exposure to the flak and fighters three times. Tonnage is not the be-all and end-all if, for instance, you can bring higher levels of accuracy into the equation; but given European flying weather as mentioned, that too was problematic.

A lot of B-17s were produced by Boeing and this at least made possible a quantitative contribution to countering lower bomb-loads. They were indeed operated in big numbers. Boeing made a total of over 12,500 B-17s during the war and, as Operation Pointblank – the directive to concentrate on destroying the Luftwaffe – gained traction, Boeing was eventually able to produce replacements at twice the rate they were being shot down. This meant that the inventory was at its fullest at the end of the war, an impressive reversal in net attrition rate. The Consolidated Aircraft Corporation was performing similarly, working up to producing ten B-24 Liberators every day and a total of over 18,000 by the end of the war. These industrial capabilities had a truly indispensable strategic impact.

Strategy was, as it always is, a numbers game, in this example sometimes referred to as the 'Battle of the Factories'. The airfield building programme was part of this battle. Parallel with the building programme there had to be a supporting supply network providing the vast range and quantity of required materiel on time and to the right place. Most of it had to be shipped across the Atlantic, 3,000 miles of sea crossing made hazardous by U-boat attacks. This was an enormous and ongoing exercise in the newly emergent science of Logistics. The Allies, incomparably the Americans, used the latest technology in manufacturing processes to increase output, which continued to climb throughout the war. The United States did this in other strategically important areas such as prefabricated ship construction. Industrial processes were key parts of the plan that eventually enabled strategic bombing to dislocate and disrupt the output of German industry. Without detracting one iota from the bravery of the young aircrew, the brilliance of US industrial process designers and the managers who put them to work contributed critically to the Allies' ability to prevail.

But things did not start nearly as well as hoped. The work-up phase must have included specialized tactics such as massive formation flying with huge aircraft and use of the Norden sight to control the aircraft track over the ground via the autopilot on a separate individual basis on the final stages of bombing runs. The collision risk must have been evident enough, yet apparently not immediately acted upon. Overestimation of the ability of the bomber formations to defend themselves once they had flown beyond the extreme radius of action of Allied fighters persisted. Many bomber commanders still expressed doubt about the use and necessity of escorting fighters at all. Was it the case that, at the very top, these eventualities with all their risk were quietly faced as a price that had to be paid? Were they brushed aside because no alternative to daylight bombing could be entertained in order to take advantage of the accuracy of the Norden sight? Regarding that, it was no secret that European weather was notoriously inclement and that for seven months of the year the ability to see the ground from high altitude was the exception as much as the rule. The RAF had been air fighting for over two years and was an invaluable source of tactical and operational experience, but their warnings were set aside. It was one thing to choose to set aside the advice of an ally; but if that meant that the first time your tactics were tested in battle was against a foe as ferociously effective as the Luftwaffe, you were dicing with the devil.

Chapter 7

Dicing With the Devil

The B-17s crews had been awoken in the early hours of the morning to prepare for the day. After washing, they walked to a briefing tent where the target would be revealed. The navigators went into a huddle and discussed weather, routing, made calculations and noted everything down. They assembled at their aeroplane to help ready it and carry out pre-start checks. Eventually a flare was fired by the air traffic control tower – the order to start engines. Sixty Wright radial engines screeched, coughed, flamed unburned fuel, and after more complaint and back-firing, burst into life shattering the quiet of the dark of the early Suffolk morning.

After completing pre-flight checks, the captain returned the salute of the ground crew and, one by one, in their allotted turns, the aircraft started to move off chocks. The pilots wore their peaked hats. They became crumpled by the earphones and stained by the sweat of tension. There was such a thing as a ten-mission hat. Less commonly, such a thing as a twenty-mission hat. Full tour twenty-five-mission hats were rare and getting rarer. The few that achieved them went home to places with names like Chicago, Illinois, or Omaha, Nebraska; changed men, older than their ages.

Within 30 minutes they were all airborne and climbing away. Large, close packed formations take time to launch, climb to height and assemble at the designated altitude before setting heading. They also became conspicuous on radar, which, as had been discovered by reconnaissance sorties, the Luftwaffe had set up. So the Luftwaffe had plenty of notice that an attack was pending.

East Anglia, and indeed England itself, took their names from the Angles from Angelin on the north Germania-Jutland border, who, with the Saxons from what is now Schleswig-Holstein, invaded and settled most of former Roman Britain. From the 5th to the 11th centuries, these 'Anglo-Saxons' tilled the land and fought off other tribes who tried to displace them. East Anglia divided itself into two counties called after 'the north folk', and 'the south folk'. Norfolk and Suffolk. These were, and continued to be, largely agrarian English counties, up before dawn to feed animals, harness horses and eat a big breakfast to prepare for a hard day's work in the fields. They sometimes went out from their barns and kitchens as dawn broke and turned their faces skyward. They watched and listened in awed curiosity as hundreds of huge bomber aircraft came into view shortly after taking off from the bases that seemed to be everywhere. On clear days the bombers would start to contrail at high altitude, the hot combustions of the big radial engines blasting out exhaust vapour, which almost instantly froze into white ice crystals. These long silver lines, highly visible against the azure sky, were man-made cirrus clouds and rather beautiful.

Cirrus clouds often precede a nice day, but these cirrus clouds indicated anything but.

The Luftwaffe was also watching – on radar but also visually. The American contrails were unavoidably marking their exact positions, visible for more than thirty miles in any direction. The altitude at which the contrails appeared varied with ambient temperature. RAF Mosquito and Spitfire reconnaissance pilots would climb until their rear-view mirrors showed they had started to contrail. The pilot would then push the stick forward into a shallow dive until the contrails vanished in the mirror, and level out. Often painted sky blue, these reconnaissance aircraft were now invisible; and invisible was good when you were armed only with cameras. This technique was not an option if your aircraft was part of a B-17 formation.

The B-17 had no home comforts. The noise levels were shattering despite intercom headsets and the body of the aircraft vibrated, shook, and lurched constantly. The mid-area of their fuselages were open to the elements to accommodate defensive guns. The Air Gunners, despite electric thermal suits and body armour that weighed over 40lbs, still experienced terrible cold and frostbite. There was, of course, oxygen at those altitudes, delivered via full-cover sculpted face masks which, with their steel helmets, made them look like something out of a sci-fi horror film. The oxygen had to be connected and flow-checked before exceeding 10,000ft. The planes were not pressurised, however; the debilitating miseries of altitude sickness had to be endured.

From American fighter bases in Suffolk, P-47 Thunderbolt fighter aircraft were taxiing towards their respective holding points to await air traffic clearance to enter the runway and take-off. Designed and built by the Republic Aircraft Company, the P-47 had many fine qualities such as speed, especially in a dive, and resistance to battle damage; but it wasn't pretty. The pilots used to call it 'The Jug'. More to the point, it was very heavy – twice as heavy as a Spitfire. With its weight and the flat frontal plan, unavoidable with big air-cooled radial engines, it produced a lot of drag, which gobbled up a lot of fuel. There was inevitably a performance price to pay for such characteristics, and the price was range and radius of action. The Thunderbolt was unable to escort the B-17s it was supposed to be protecting outbound, over the target and back again. So now there was going to be yet another enactment of the same ghastly charade. The B-17s were to be escorted by fighters that could only protect them for part of the way to the target – the part which was beyond the reach of the Luftwaffe anyway. When they had reached the limit of that radius of action, the Thunderbolts had to turn and return to base leaving the bombers to fly on into increasing levels of vulnerability alone. This is what the Luftwaffe was waiting for. By radar blip and on a clear day by contrail patterns they knew exactly when and where to pounce.

The B-17s had no protection in the final phases of the flight to the target, the attack phase and the initial phase back. These were the phases where they desperately needed it. The Luftwaffe fighters, the Me 109s, the Focke-Wulf 190s, wreaked havoc. If they received escort on the way home, it was within the segment of the sortie where they didn't need it because the Luftwaffe fighters by that time were also returning to base. An eight per cent loss rate might be deemed 'sustainable' and therefore acceptable; but such statistics have human emotion leached out of them. Eight per cent of a 500-bomber raid was still forty planes destroyed. More importantly it meant 400 crew killed, maimed, missing in action, taken POW, or evading capture in a forest somewhere being hunted down by soldiers or angry citizens. This was repeated day after day.

The German fighter controllers, monitoring the levels of radio activity and tracking the formations on radar, received adequate warning that big formations were assembling and knew that a raid was coming. They had direction detection capability and a guessing game commenced as to where the raid would attack and which formations might be feints to cause confusion. For up to an hour little happened. At the end of this time the number of possible targets had been reduced, and as the bombers droned towards them, the appropriate fighter sectors were alerted. The pilots would man the planes, start up, warm up, check all systems and instruments were serviceable, shut down again, and wait, strapped into the cockpit harness.

The bomber formations thundered on eastward. Eventually it became clear in which area the attack would take place and the defending fighter sectors ordered their squadrons into the air. The rush to get up was timed to bring the fighters into interception positions as the bombers passed at minimum distance from the fighter bases, high above the formations and, if possible, in an up-sun position. The squadron leaders of Messerschmitt 109s and Focke-Wulf 190s would pick one of the B-17 formations, peel off and lead their pilots in a dive into the attack.

The fighter is vibrating now. The controls are becoming heavy. You are aiming at the earth at over 400mph – over three times as fast as you fall when you bail out. The engine is roaring. You are only vaguely aware of this, but sufficiently aware to flick your eyes onto the engine revolutions tachometer and to see the needle is firmly in the red arc. You pull the throttle back thankful that the engine didn't reward your ham-fistedness by firing a piston out of the engine block. You are gulping oxygen. On the way down in the dive, the focus shifts from the whole formation to an individual plane within it, preferably on the periphery of the formation where the concentration of defending machine-gun fire was at a minimum. This is no time to sneeze or get a bout of eye-watering. The controls become heavier as the plane falls. In the last few seconds there are final adjustments using all controls including rudder to keep the gun-sight pip on the growing bomber. The machine gun bullets flick past, sometimes so close you flinch. The aircraft now begins to behave unpredictably, slightly kicking and jerking, and you know, against all your instincts, you must ease further back on the throttle to stabilise control. The jerking is caused by compressibility where airflow over the wing surfaces gets near to design limits. If this is not corrected in time the extreme manifestation is 'control reversal' where the aircraft reacts exactly opposite to the pilot's control inputs, which is not only nerve-wracking but makes it nearly impossible to aim. The gunsight is still off a bit but that's as good as it's going to get so you press the firing button. The sound of firing overrides everything else as you watch your tracer shells in relation to the track of your quarry. Are they striking home? Your vision blurs. You hold the firing button for as long as you dare then pull, pull away. Into the vertical, into the sun, anything to get out of it. The airspeed falls off rapidly. You cough into your oxygen mask which immediately blows your spit back into your face. The airspeed is now dropping below 200mph and you need to get a grip. You look over your shoulder to chandelle turn with the propeller torque. Where the hell did they go? Then suddenly you see them again, still flying serenely on towards Berlin as though nothing had happened! It is hard to believe. All this effort and I am not making any difference here. With exasperation rising in your throat you tell yourself to stop over-controlling while bringing the fighter around and into another dive. The nose goes down, shallower this time because the American formation is now over three miles away. The throttle goes fully open and once again the engine starts to wail…

Fighter pilots kept up the fighter's advantageous high energy by pulling the attacking dive back into a high-speed climb, re-acquiring the formation below visually and diving down again onto another target bomber. These manoeuvres were continual, but each dive had to face the guns of the formation. An alternative tactic was to intercept at a point in front of the formation and, either singly or in groups, to make a frontal attack. Regrouping to carry out each of a series of these horizontal attacks took more time as the fighters had to reverse direction, overtake the formation above and re-position, but frontal attacks were terrifyingly effective, and the bombers had hardly any forward-facing guns to return fire.

From the point of view of the bomber crews, fighter aircraft were tiny things not much bigger than a dot as they closed in and hard to pick out, especially as they had the habit of deliberately lining themselves up between the sun and their targets. A very fast attack, out of the blinding sun in the freezing blue skies at 25,000ft, posed big problems for air gunners. There was a blast of bullets or, much worse, cannon shells ripping great, jagged chucks of the outer fuselage away or exploding inside it. Rupturing a key system such as the hydraulics would manifest itself in the immediate onset of handling problems while the pilots commenced a struggle to hold position within the formation. Internal explosions for whatever reason could kill or maim any crewmember within the compartment. If they hit a fuel tank, it was probably all over. They contained, not paraffin as with the later jets; not diesel fuel as with agricultural machines; it was petrol, or as Americans called it, 'gas' – short for gasoline – the same as you put into your automobile. It had a flashpoint so low you could set it off lighting a cigarette.

The bomb groups, locked together in tight formation, were all committed to maintaining a steady course while being attacked by demons, silent under the roar of their own engines. Each crew member stood a high chance of becoming a casualty. If you were killed, that was that; but if you were wounded you had to self-doctor, but there was a limit to what you could do if it was even slightly serious. If, as likely, you were losing blood, you had very little time in which to do it before you lost consciousness and shortly afterwards you were dead. Some deaths were slow and agonising. Machine-gun bullets could rip off a limb while leaving you alive. One was enough. An exploding cannon shell could spell the end for everything alive inside the fuselage. Rocket firing Me 109s were the worst threat of all. A frontal hit by a rocket could disrupt the entire plane as a viable entity in a split second. If you were not going down in flames yourself you could see many that were and knew that the next attack might inflict the same fate on you and your crew. All that is to say little of the fear and dread you were feeling and having to carry on regardless. Do your job.

If you got through to the target, strangely, fighter attacks suddenly calmed down. The Krupps 88mm flak guns were concentrated on the approaches to strategic targets to defend them and the Luftwaffe pilots didn't want to be anywhere near what was about to happen. The USAAF planes were bombing from lower levels than the extremes the RAF was playing with at the time, but that came at a nasty price. In the run-up and fly-away from the target it put them right over those seemingly ubiquitous flak guns, which would destroy any aircraft they hit. But the fighters had gone for now. The gunners scooped hundreds of clips and empty shell cases out of the open hatches.

They connected new ammunition belts to the guns, which were almost red-hot and still smoking even in the freezing slipstream.

The flak storm began as the B-17s arrived over the gun battery rings surrounding the target, and which began to exact a further toll in bombers and crews. In this predicament there was not even the few seconds' warning of an attacking fighter. If you were hit by an 88mm shell shard there was a bang and immediate consequences in the constitution and behaviour of the aircraft. If you were hit directly by a flak shell there was a mind-shattering explosion which, if you were not killed outright, might leave you badly injured or stunned and paralysed with shock, unable to help yourself or anyone else. The two pilots were the critical issue, but there was no way yet devised not to put them right at the front of the plane. One left alive was usually enough if he wasn't injured too badly and the plane was still flyable.

The navigator in the lead aircraft checked the formation's position and passed a precise time over target (TOT) to the bombardier, who started running checks on his Norden bombsight. He checked data for altitude, pressure, average wind vector below the aircraft, temperature, and true airspeed. Track adjustments were fed directly into the bomber's autopilot and the pilots went hands off. During the run into the target, after Curtis LeMay's changes to procedure, only the lead aircraft was flying using the Norden sight connected to the automatic pilot to maintain the track on the bombing run. The device was a big advance in bombing technology – in good weather. All the other aircraft crews were now forbidden to do this too as the technique was deemed to incur too high a risk of mid-air collisions. 'Blue on blue', 'own goals' – call them what you like – they were the most tragic of events. The other aircraft were being hand-flown by the pilots to maintain station.

The final adjustments had to be made with the whole formation running in straight and level making things simpler for anyone who was trying to hit them with guns. Radio silence was maintained between the aircraft in the formation. If damage had been caused by a hit, the engineer checked the gauges for signs of damage and the state of the rear crew inside the fuselage. The flak intensified. Only one shell in ten fired from the 88mm guns on the ground was a tracer shell. The airmen hated to remind themselves that for every tracer they could see there were nine behind it that were invisible. The shells burst short – below them – to begin with. But soon the gunners had adjusted the gun elevations and the carnage began again. This time the bombers had no reply – they had simply to grit teeth and drive on through it. More of the formation were lost. No time to think about that because the target was coming up.

The bombardiers opened the bomb doors when they saw the lead-aircraft bomb doors open. The bombs were checked visually to confirm that they were primed. Then they looked left or right at the lead aircraft. In the lead aircraft the target slid down the aiming graticule and at the exactly calculated moment, the bomb release was triggered. The bomber lurched upwards as its load suddenly lightened by 2 tons. Seeing bombs falling from the lead aircraft, all the other bombardiers released their bombloads, and all the other crews felt the same upward lurch together. The doors were closed and the pilots maintained heading waiting for the photograph to show exactly where the bombs had struck. There could be no hard breaks to port or starboard. Position in formation had to be maintained as the whole squadron, or what was left of it, started to manoeuvre in a dangerously stately, gentle turn to start the journey back to base. Clear of the target area there was about half an hour's calm. The squadron flew on, this time westward.

* * *

After half an hour of tense frantic duelling, the Luftwaffe fighters had run low on fuel and one by one broke out of the battle to return to base. Now, the headphones were full of talk, shouted warnings, commands, curses and sometimes, somehow most ominously – silence. An Me 109 pilot, who only eighteen months ago had left school, pushed up his goggles, which had clouded. He wiped his eyes with the back of his glove. He drew a deep breath and held it for seconds before exhaling. He switched his radio to the recovery radio frequency and left the mayhem behind. He was in a slight daze which was pleasant because, for now, he was out of it. The Controller gave him heading and range for base and began talking to another aircraft. He was dismissed and found his own way home. He got to 2,000ft over his base aerodrome and entered the circuit aiming to follow another Me 109 in front of him. He descended and turned less than half a mile behind him matching the aircraft in front in a 70-degree banked turn into the downwind position, ignoring standard procedure not to apply more than 45 degrees of bank after battle in case of insidious damage to the aircraft. Everyone did. He checked his speed and height, lowered flap and undercarriage when prompted to do so by mimicking the Me 109 in front. He then sat line astern on his unwitting partner, just keeping him at the same range and same position in the windscreen, and relaxed. Then, the one in front rolled to the right towards the base leg of the circuit and began to sink. The pilot glanced at the base leg and approach, which had another Me 109 on final approach near to landing but another 109 joining for a straight in approach. This complicated things, so he maintained height and extended his downwind leg watching as his former lead aircraft dropped away down to his right. Good luck sorting that one out, Mein Herr! After counting to ten and scrutinising again for other aircraft that might be joining for a straight in approach, he didn't mess about. There was his hole in the pattern, and he rolled right, half closed the throttle, and kept scanning for others. On the base leg with the aerodrome at half right he was still too high, so he eased in top rudder and deliberately put his aircraft out of balance into a sideslip. The excess height disappeared as if by magic and he rolled level looking for a green light from the tower. The touchdown was clumsy because his hands were shaking with stress. He turned off the runway quickly enough not to balk any aircraft coming in to land behind him, but not quickly enough to rip off his own tyres. That was frowned upon. He taxied back to dispersal. The manual recommended a fast walking speed for taxiing, but manuals are not written for when people are trying to bomb your airfield. The OK buzz was that if your Air Speed Indicator is still indicating zero, it's acceptable, which produced some exciting taxi speeds when downwind. To avoid nosing over you needed to pull your joystick well back into your groin. He spared himself recalling the ribald crew-room humour about that – he'd heard it all before.

He entered dispersal under the control of a Feldwebel's quickly gesticulating hands. He held her on brakes as chocks were inserted and closed the fuel cock. The propeller eventually became visible and stopped. Immediately the engine began to clack as it started to cool. There were twenty-eight post flight actions, switches, levers, to carry out. Before he had finished the Feldwebel was already on his wing pushing open the hood.

'Are you all right, Herr Leutnant?'
'Fine, thank you.'
'Anything wrong with the aircraft?'
'No, she's just fine. Thank you.'

He looked at him and nodded. The Feldwebel nodded back and sat on the spine as the pilot slid off the wing and unstrapped his parachute, threw it over his shoulder and walked towards the Ops building. On entering he was greeted by an Operations Officer.

'Any kills?'

'Don't know. It was a frontal – only seconds between firing and pulling out – no time to see what damage was done if any. I pulled up and looked back, but there were so many of them trailing smoke I can't even be sure which one I attacked to be honest. Got in another one – same result.'

'All right, I'll record two 'probables', and, by the way, this has nothing to do with honesty. Everything to do with public morale. You can be sure they're doing the same over there. Some of the claims they're making on the BBC make me laugh out loud. They claimed they'd bombed Bottrop night before last. It was news to Bottrop – they reported a quiet night's sleep. Go and get a coffee and something to eat. You'll be up again in an hour or so no doubt'.

The pilot had a pee, smoked a cigarette made from God knows what, and a cup of ersatz coffee, the best that ground acorns could produce. By the end of the week all details of that engagement were lost to memory, confused with a dozen more recent but similar engagements. In the crew-room the less experienced pilots chatted together comparing notes and explaining their aerial manoeuvres with their hands. The more experienced dozed in their chairs, grateful for a few minutes' oblivion.

Eventually, in the Luftwaffe sector bases, the bell rang again. The pilots tumbled out of the standby room door leaving half-full mugs of acorn coffee and lit cigarettes in ash trays and ran towards their now refuelled and rearmed fighters. Up onto the wing, hands on both runnels of the cockpit hood and lift both feet into the cockpit. The armourer drops the straps over the pilot's shoulders and jumps off the wing. Then everything pauses for a few moments. One by one the engines coughed, blew out fuel vapour in a white cloud, and roared into life. Within minutes the squadron is bumping over the grass towards the take-off assembly point. They are cleared to take-off in battle pairs, and after take-off two pairs form up into a *schwarm* of four. The *schwarms* climbed at full throttle while being vectored to intercept the returning B-17 formations from a position with the sun behind them and in the eyes of their quarries. Almost impossible to make them out. They don't quite make the optimum altitude to begin the attack, but it is enough. They gain visual contact with the returning American planes, manoeuvre, peel off, dive, select a single aircraft, open fire and the carnage begins again.

Twenty minutes of high 'g' turns later and soaked in sweat, one of the four fighters is shot down. Trying to position for a head-on attack, he turns in far too high and is caught squarely by the dorsal gunners from three B-17s. All three gunners made a claim to have shot it down. There was nothing disingenuous about this over-claiming. There may be many guns hammering away at a single aircraft, but each gunner, only aware of his own shooting, if he sees the plane he is firing at suddenly burst into flames will naturally assume it fell to his guns. Such multi-claiming was commonplace but could not be prevented. Over-claiming had a good side. If the gunners had known how little damage they were really inflicting on the Luftwaffe it would, without a doubt, have had powerfully lowering effect on an already precarious general morale, and all that comes with that.

Then, another of the *schwarm* loses its engine, which blows a gasket at the top of one full-throttle climb too many. His airspeed falling off rapidly; he feels a crash behind him and a sharp pain in his back and he knows he has been caught by a burst of machine gun fire. He leans forward in his seat straps and puts his left hand behind him and rubs the spot. He pulls his hand back and looks at his gauntlet. There is no blood. Good. It was just a belt in the back then. If there had been enemy fighters about, the pilot of that aircraft would have dived to get out of the battle area or possibly bailed out. But there were no enemy fighters. The British and Americans had no single-engine fighters that could range this far out from their bases; and twin-engine types such as the Mosquito and the P-38 Lightning did not have the dog-fighting manoeuvrability to take on the Me 109 or the Fw 190. The Luftwaffe knew this.

In a dive to get away and below the battle, he calmly stop-cocks the engine as a fire precaution, selects a stage of flap to lower the nose to increase forward visibility and reduce his stalling speed, and starts looking for suitable area to carry out an engine-out landing. For the first time, with his silent aircraft, he can hear the rattle of machine guns and the scream of tortured engines above him and it seems strange to be able to do so.

He slows to a fast glide. The silent Me 109 took over ten minutes to get down to around 3,000ft where the decision about where you were going to try to land became all-absorbing. But the pilot had seen it already from 5,000ft – it was obvious. It was a long narrow field, over half a mile long in fact, close to a road and a village. He was far too high, but not so high that he could risk a full 360-degree circle. That would put him too low. He looked at the drift on his nose. It was right to left so the wind was from the right. He turned the Messerschmitt to put the field in his right 2 o'clock. He now had a base-leg turn to play with and that made height management easier on an engine-out approach. He was still too high, even aiming one third into the selected field for landing to avoid bashing into the near hedge at 120mph. Better to over-roll and clout the far hedge at 30mph. That was survivable. He lowered his undercarriage and selected full flap to increase drag and rate of descent and threw in a couple of S-turns to add to the height loss. At 200ft it all came right. He centralised the controls and for the first time stopped pushing her nose down. The Me 109 raised her nose like the thoroughbred she was and settled gently onto the grass in a perfect three-point landing.

He didn't apply brake. He was having a good time. It was as though he were not part of it. It was as if his aeroplane knew what she was doing and what was required of her, so she did it all by herself. She stopped. He pulled back the hood. The engine was cracking as it cooled; but high above his head he could hear a lark singing. He put his head back and listened and smiled. It felt surreal. Here he was, feeling happy listening to birdsong, when 20 minutes ago he was being crushed by 6g of gravity, firing guns, trying to kill people who were trying to kill him. He decided that he liked it better down here.

He groped for a cigarette but couldn't find them. He thought to himself that he felt a bit drunk. He somehow didn't feel inclined to climb out of the aircraft. He was comfortable where he was. From the far end of the field there came a horse with a small dray, high stepping towards him. They stopped and a man jumped out.

'Hello. Are you ok?'
'Yes, of course. Thank you.'

The man leapt onto the wing. He looked at the pilot's rank.

'You should get out of this plane, Herr Leutnant. There is a strong smell of gasoline.'
'Yes, of course.'

He attempted to get out of the seat and failed.

'Wait – wait, Herr Leutnant. You must release your harness.'
'Ah, yes, of course. How foolish.'

The man reached in and released his harness. He helped him to stand, then one leg after the other, helped him out on to the wing, where he lost consciousness and collapsed, falling over the trailing edge and onto the ground on his face. The whole of the back of his flying suit was soaked in blood. Other people arrived, out of breath. Panting, they lifted the unconscious pilot onto the dray and the horse was whipped towards the doctor's house. The doctor had been alerted by the general kerfuffle in the village and heaved himself onto the cart. He put his fingers to the pilot's jugular vein and his spectacles under his nose for signs of heart and breath. He turned to the small crowd and said,

'I am sorry. He is dead. He lost too much blood. There is nothing I can do for him.'

The small crowd uttered a low moan. A little girl began to cry.
She was only just turned five, but already, and before she should, she knew what the word *'tot'* meant.
The losses to the squadrons of B-17s on the way back to England had been harrowing. The shoot-downs of B-17s continued. The German radar operator had seen returns coming east, which he knew were Allied fighters; RAF Spitfires, or P-47 Thunderbolts, putting up a perfunctory show of escorting the bombers home. He broadcasted a codeword. The Me 109s, the Fw 190s, their ammunition spent and running short of fuel now anyway, happily broke off the battle and went home.
The remaining B-17s made it back to base. On landing two more aircraft crashed on the runway due to battle damage. There are serious injuries to the crews, many corpses, many mangled

and in bits. They are wrapped in cloths and carefully lifted away to hospital or mortuary.

It is horrendous to try to envisage what it could be like to experience being cooped up in a flimsy metal box, in brain-numbing levels of noise and vibration and freezing, sub-zero temperatures, miles above the Earth, while swarms of fighters at sonic speed hurl themselves straight at you with machine-guns hammering out deadly streams of bullets and shells, every single one of which could spell a terrible end for you or your buddies. Thousands died this way. The American poet Randall Jarrell, himself an Air Force officer, wrote in 1945,

> 'From my mother's sleep I fell into the State,
> And I hunched in its belly till my wet fur froze.
> Six miles from earth, loosed from its dream of life,
> I woke to black flak and the nightmare fighters.
> When I died, they washed me out of the turret with a hose.'
>   The Death of The Ball Turret Gunner.

The airfields fall quiet in the early afternoon. The grim tragedy is repeated, day after week after month.

Of the 150 B-17s taking part in this imagined but typical raid, nineteen did not return. Four crashed on landing, and seven were damaged beyond repair and were struck off. The aircraft attrition rate was 20 per cent – deemed unsustainable. Of 1,500 aircrew, there were 247 aircrew casualties. Forty-seven were killed and some became prisoners of war. Nine were never accounted for.

General Ira Eaker stuck to the doctrine, believing that it was right but only if the force was determined enough to persist with it for long enough. By the end of the strategic air war in Europe, 47,000 Americans out of 115,000 were casualties, including more than 26,000 dead. In over 440,000 bomber sorties 700,000 tons of bombs were dropped, with 5,100 aircraft losses. General Eaker was eventually replaced by others similarly minded.

Chapter 8

Gaining Altitude

In the face of such costly tragedy, an increasing conviction grew, reluctantly in some, that the only answer to the problem of unsustainable losses of bombers and crews was effective escort fighter protection, outbound, over the target, and on the return to base. This was easier said than done. The single-engine fighters currently operated by the Allies did not have the range to do this. Twin-engine fighters had the radius of action but not the agility to prevail in an open fight against the single-engine Me 109 and certainly not against the new pugnacious Focke-Wulf 190. This is why the Luftwaffe had lost so many Me 110 twin fighters in the Battle of Britain – they could not match the manoeuvrability of Hurricanes and Spitfires. The Allies needed a fighter that could do both. The search was on, but it was a tall order. Was such a thing possible at all?

Everything in the aircraft type inventory was re-considered, including the Allison-engined Mustang. The Allison engine was optimised for lower altitudes, and below 20,000ft was a capable fighter – indeed had been outstanding in that role. As described, the RAF used it for combined operations with ground forces providing armed reconnaissance, ground attack and army co-operation sorties. Superchargers had been developed primarily to maintain the power output of piston aero engines as they climbed for height, but with an aircraft that was optimised for low to medium level combat this was not critical. The Allison engine had a single stage of supercharging, which was adequate for combat below 20,000ft, so this engine was a good choice for the original specification. However, as the war progressed, the heights at which battles were taking place inexorably increased. Lacking high-level supercharging initially seemed to rule the Mustang out. It would not have been long before Luftwaffe fighter pilots noticed that, in a medium level dogfight, pulling for height was the answer to an attacking Mustang. Twenty thousand feet and above would be a safe-haven for Me 109s and Fw 190s, from where they could set up a diving attack with impunity, followed by a zoom-climb to above 20,000ft and relative safety again. *Wunderbar*!

Royal Air Force Fighter Command rejected the Allison Mustang for their use. It was a matter of unchallengeable, tactical doctrine that gaining higher altitude than your foe was indispensable for successful engagement. This prevailed at the time, even though many Spitfires were being shot down from below and behind, as fitting bubble canopies later revealed. No question in anyone's mind at the time though – you had to attack at high speed in a dive from above, and an aircraft that ran out of performance above 20,000ft would not do.

'Supercharging' is a generic term comprising both superchargers and turbo-superchargers. Supercharging in aeroengines was developed to counteract the reduction of engine-power output in piston engines as the air thinned when the aircraft climbed. They are basically powerful air compressors. The main difference between the two is that whereas superchargers are driven as an accessory from the engine crankshaft, turbo-superchargers are driven by a high-speed gas turbine, itself driven by the high-pressure exhaust gases as they are expelled from the exhaust manifold. For this reason, its name is often abbreviated to simply 'turbocharger'. Of the two types, the turbocharger is the more efficient. The exhaust gases are hot and expelled at high pressure but, if the Meredith Effect is ignored, are just wasted energy in a normally aspirated engine. The turbocharger harnesses them and puts their energy to good use by increasing the mass flow of induction mixture, something it achieves at no extra cost. The thermal efficiency of the engine therefore increases. The normal supercharger, being driven from the crankshaft, is using energy that could have been made available to the propellor. The thermal efficiency of a supercharged engine therefore actually decreases. Turbochargers were coming into play although they were bulky. Lockheed P-36 Lightnings had the fuselage room, and its engines were turbocharged. B-17 Wright Cyclone engines were also turbocharged. They applied themselves to augmenting this advantage in other ways. The engine cooling intake, set far back below the fuselage, was also optimised for the lowest drag possible. It made a further and clever contribution by heating the intake air within the cooling radiator so that it expanded and then constricting its exit from the aircraft using convergent exhausts. This increased the speed of the expelling air providing a small but significant amount of jet thrust. Named the Meredith Effect after its British inventor, the thrust added some 10–12 mph to the aircraft's forward speed. A similar effect was gained by fitting special exhausts to another aircraft – the de Havilland Mosquito. It was not unique, but it was a savvy bit of development. Taken all together the design added to the aircraft's top speed with commensurate advantage to climb performance as well as range.

American engineers had been to the fore of supercharger development since shortly after the First World War. They were therefore well placed to understand the limitations of normally aspirated or under-supercharged aero engines as they climbed to increasing altitudes. Some commentaries imply that the selection of the Allison engine was an error on the part of the American P-51 designers. This is untrue. The original British specification, centred on army cooperation, required a low-to-medium altitude, ground-attack fighter where a high level of forced induction was not critical. The British got what the British had asked for. The Allison Mustang gave them unparalleled performance in the tactical role they had in mind.

Why was the strategic potential of this aeroplane not recognised sooner? It might to come down to the notion that the answer you get depends on the question you ask, and whether you are open-minded about innovative or unconventional possibilities. If you ask whether the Allison Mustang could serve as a high-altitude fighter, the answer is going to be no, but you have obtained the right answer to the wrong question. What if a more open question had been asked?

The Mustang was all but ruled out, but further opinions were sought to see if any possibility had been missed or whether someone could come up with some lateral thinking. This is the stuff of legend. Rolls-Royce test pilot Ronald Harker returned from a test flight of the Allison Mustang with guarded praise for the type. In the post-flight debriefing the altitude limitations were discussed, at the end of which Harker chose to summarise the problem by saying the aircraft was impressive in terms of the airframe aerodynamics but dogged by the wrong power plant. His conclusion was that there was nothing amiss with this plane that fitting a Rolls-Royce Merlin engine wouldn't put right.

It should have been a eureka moment, but when Rolls-Royce gave the proposal voice, it was met with distinct reluctance on the part of the RAF and some government officials. They worried that the supply of British-made Merlins would run short of demand. After all, it was the engine of choice for Supermarine's Spitfire, Hawker's Hurricane, de Havilland's Mosquito and Avro's Lancaster. These were Britain's top class war planes and there was a war on. None to waste on experiments. Nevertheless, a programme was drawn up and Rolls-Royce proved very persistent. It was therefore agreed that two-stage, two-speed, supercharged Merlins could be made available to test on Mustang airframes, and the tests would go ahead at the end of

1942. The doubters believed and hoped that the tests would fail and that would be the end of a tiresome distraction.

The Merlin Mustang test programme began, flown by Rolls-Royce's chief test pilot. The early data indicated that the results would be conclusive and beyond doubt. With the Merlin, the Mustang's performance at high altitude was no longer a weakness but would be transformed into a clear strength.

The ability of the Rolls-Royce Merlin engine to breathe success into a failing project was nothing new. Avro in Britain experienced a similar situation with a new, twin-engine bomber they were prototyping, which they called the Avro Manchester. The two 24-cylinder Vulture engines had caused endless trouble including failing and even catching fire. Abandoning this line of development, they fitted four Merlins instead and immediately found they had a winner on their hands. They called it the Lancaster.

The RAF was still not sufficiently convinced to proceed with installing it in the Mustang, so attention was turned towards the USA. North American Aviation of Los Angeles, California (NAA) received from the US Embassy in London and from Rolls-Royce, information about the success of the trials of the Merlin Mustang. Rolls-Royce accompanied this with performance data showing that the top speed of the new fighter would be over 430mph. North American carried out tests of its own on two aircraft with Merlin engines obtained from Packard of Detroit, Michigan, which was producing them under licence from Rolls-Royce. Having verified the data, they abandoned the Allison engine altogether, fitting Merlins to their brand-new Mustangs and Merlin Mustangs went into immediate production. These Mustangs now had the ability to climb robustly to over 30,000ft and had come of age as a true all-altitude dogfighter.

Overcoming the altitude limitations in the Mustang was achieved, albeit belatedly, by appropriate super-charging and this gave the Allies an all-new technology fighter to add to the inventory. But as Churchill said,

> *'The Fighters are our salvation…but* the *Bombers* alone provide the means of victory.'

Only bomber aircraft, ran the argument, with the strategic capability of attacking the enemy's infrastructure, industrial capacity and population – the capacity to wage war at all – could deliver victory and win the war. This, to the strategic bombing 'mafia', would have sounded like a re-endorsement of Douhet's theories. The proponents of integrated combined operations on the other hand, would have interpreted this as nice rhetoric, but it did not preclude their conviction that strategic bombing was not a war-winner on its own. They viewed it as necessary but insufficient for victory. In the event, through the insistence of Supreme Commander Eisenhower and the persuasiveness of Deputy Supreme Commander Tedder, the latter doctrine prevailed.

The essential components of a successful strategic bombing capability remained as they always were – bomber range sufficient to reach the target and return to a base; bomber survivability keeping losses within sustainable limits; an efficacious total weight of bombs dropped accurately on the target. The B-17 achieved the range criterion but only at the expense bomb-weight criterion. Without fighter cover it did not, and could not, achieve the survivability requirement.

Regarding fighters, the first requirement was for an escort fighter with the range of a bomber; a fighter with fuel sufficient to protect the bombers in both transit legs and over the target. Secondly it had to be blessed with outstanding manoeuvrability to take on the Fw 190. The new formula would be a partnership between 'Big Friends' and 'Little Friends'.

Having solved the Mustang's altitude issue, such possibilities began to suggest themselves. The Mustang began to look as though it might become something much more than an excellent, tactical weapon. For this to happen however, the issue of range and radius of action of the aircraft was still to be addressed.

Chapter 9

A Fighter with the Range of a Bomber

Neither RAF Fighter Command, nor the US Eighth Army Air Force had an aircraft type that would allow unescorted, deep-penetration raids in daylight on German strategic targets. Consequently, the bomber force continued to take punishment beyond bearing. Faith in the self-sufficiency of the armed bomber formation, in the face of the figures, was discredited. Bombers could not achieve air superiority – only fighters could do that. The Luftwaffe had prevailed. They retained not just air superiority over Germany, but air supremacy. It was their sky, and if you flew into it you ran a big risk of being shot down. Unescorted bombing over Germany was suspended in October 1943.

Protection of bombers by long-range fighters was no longer contentious. It was now regarded as key. Such fighters would have to carry fuel for a radius of action enabling them to fly top-cover over the bomber formations throughout their long return journeys; and manoeuvrability to shoot down attacking Luftwaffe fighters on the outbound leg, over the target, and all the way home again until the B-17s touched down in England.

Existing fighters were tactical and defensive, or in some cases tactical and offensive; but they always lacked the magic combination of single-engine manoeuvrability with deep-penetration range. Some had one, and some had the other; but none had both. They were good at the job they had been designed for but did not have the range of a bomber.

It was even tougher than that. With the high probability of dogfights during the outbound, over-target and return phases, the fuel also needed to be sufficient to supply significant periods of time with the engine at combat throttle settings when the fuel consumption was prodigious.

As options were eliminated, the Mustang started to look like a possibility. The new slippery laminar-flow technology in P-51s had produced a low-drag coefficient, fuel-efficient contender, and assisted with Meredith effect jet propulsion, had a good radius of action. It offered hope.

What was the magic of laminar flow? Why did it make such a difference to a fighter aircraft? It was envisaged as a way of overcoming the neglected problem of aerodynamic drag. The engine and propeller of an aircraft develop thrust by propelling a large mass of air rearwards. The aircraft reacts to this by moving forward, the same principle as an oar in the water. This is sometimes called The Law of Action and Reaction, or Newton's Third Law. Thrust, or forward propulsion, must overcome drag, which is the resistance of the air through which the aircraft is flying. A thick object, in this case a wing, will produce more drag than a thin. This will be readily understood by comparing how it feels to whisk a piece of cardboard flat side on, with trying to whisk it edge side on.

In addition, a heavy aircraft will produce more drag because it demands a greater angle of attack (the angle the wing presents to the air in forward motion) to generate sufficient lift, which produces further drag. In the conventions of aerodynamics of the time, there was no such thing as a free lunch. It just needed more thrust to overcome it. Drag was under-investigated.

The experiments began. The technologists involved had not been able to ignore that modern aircraft wings were fat. They had bulbous leading edges which were at their fattest close to the front of the wing, and this caused the smooth flow across the top surface to break down into turbulence early. Turbulent flow across most of the wing surface produced a soaring increase in drag. The wing underside in cross section was concave or slightly cup-shaped, again adding significantly to drag. Parachutes are cup-shaped to be deliberately inefficient aerodynamically. In other words, the wing design had been optimised to produce lift with less emphasis on drag reduction, relying solely on engine thrust to overcome it. To re-phrase all this pertinently, if there are two aircraft with the same engine and propeller (thrust), the one with the lesser drag will perform better – faster, further and higher.

Drag is critically limiting to aircraft performance therefore, and the problem gets worse the faster you go. In general terms, for every arithmetic increase in speed, drag increases geometrically. If you need to increase from 100mph to 200mph (x2) the increase in drag will be four-fold (x4) or 2 squared. If you want to increase from 100mph to 300mph (x3), the increase in drag will be nine-fold (x9) or 3 squared. And so on.

Approaching the problem more radically, North American Aviation had designed thin-wing alternatives, which extended the smooth boundary layer and delayed the break-away into drag-inducing turbulent flow to more than half-way towards the trailing edge of the wing. This resulted in a dramatic reduction in drag. They avoided the almost universally-adopted convex teardrop, or comma-shaped curvature of wing cross-section, substituting a wing with greatly reduced, drag-inducing camber, relying more on angle of attack to generate lift. Looked at from the side, the Mustang wing seems almost razor-like compared with those on other contemporary warplanes.

Such a wing lost effectiveness as a lift generator at low airspeeds, which in turn meant longer take-off runs and higher take-off and approach speeds. The extra risk this entailed was mitigated by installing much bigger wing flaps to reduce stalling speeds. Those barn-door flaps were useful tactically too. On a patrol, selection of small angles of flap would move the nose down increasing all-important visibility – the ability to scan the sky for the enemy and, crucially, to see him first before he saw you. That gave you some seconds to manoeuvre to gain an advantage. They could even reduce the radius of turn in a fight. The strategic Holy Grail of a combination of speed, height performance, range and manoeuvrability was starting to come together made possible by the magic of 'laminar flow'.

NAA left no stone unturned. The fighters of the time were designed in the 'taildragger' configuration. In their determination to reduce drag, the Mustang was given a retracting tailwheel, as described previously. The fuselage rivets were filed flush, further to aid a smooth, turbulent-free airflow. At the same time NAA carried out an ongoing critical design review of weight of components with an intention of reducing everything to minimum weight. This included making one component deliver more than one function, requiring very clever design. NAA ingenuity did not disappoint.

All this having been said, there could be no avoiding that the carriage of increased fuel load was crucial. At the beginning, the Mustang's range, carrying internal fuel alone, was around 1,000 miles. An extra 85-gallon internal tank was fitted into the fuselage extending the range to 1,300 miles The new aircraft was relatively lightly armed to allow an increase in the proportion of fuel within the total load. The technicians then experimented with jettisonable drop tanks made of reinforced papier-mâché, which increased the operational range to over 1,600 miles (2,500km). Further modifications, including the Malcolm bubble canopy to allow monitoring of the aircraft's 6 o'clock, pushed the range to over 2,000 miles with an endurance of 8 hours 30 minutes. This was unheard of in a single-engine fighter. It elevated the Merlin Mustang into a class of its own. There was, at last, a single-engine fighter with the range of a bomber, and the Merlin Mustang was the only one.

In February 1944, delivery of new Merlin Mustangs to the US Eighth Army Air Force in England began. The strategic air campaign in Europe was about to recommence.

Chapter 10

Air Supremacy

The Luftwaffe had anticipated an all out Allied strategic air offensive in 1941 and had set up an air-defence radar network in western Europe. They moved 160 Me 109s west and, significantly, the brand-new Fw 190, their top piston fighter. Within the USAAF, exaggerated assessments of the severity of damage being inflicted on the enemy delayed realisation that the success of the strategic bombing campaign depended on doing much more to destroy the fighter-driven air superiority still retained by the Luftwaffe deep inside Germany. This was essential, but still not accepted by the pure bomber advocates. The protagonists of the various options continued to champion their pet theories, delaying objective debate about alternatives. There is a fine line between doctrine and dogma. Making a virtue of dispensing with escort fighters to defend attacking bomber formations was on the wrong side of it.

The US 8th AAF had been given bombing target priorities in early 1943 at the Casablanca Conference, headed by Churchill and Roosevelt. Unsurprisingly, attacking U-Boat construction and aircraft production were at the top. These raised the debate to focus on the strategic, aimed at destroying the enemy's capacity to wage war at all. The raids were to begin as early as possible but the succeeding months in Europe were bad for flying with much of the effort frustrated by difficult navigational problems, cloud and fog obscuring target areas, or base conditions so bad that take-offs were delayed waiting for an improvement in the weather that never came. On sorties where attacking U-boat pens was a reasonable prospect, the tactical improvement in the Luftwaffe formations that opposed them became all too apparent. The defenders were still strongly contesting the air superiority battle. In the spring of 1943, a raid was directed at the Focke-Wulf factories at Bremen south-west of Schleswig-Holstein in northern Germany. Carrying out well-rehearsed tactics, wave after wave of German fighters positioned themselves to attack the USAAF bombers. They were akin to aerial firing squads. The bombers were flying together in huge, close formations, lining up on the target run where the possibility of manoeuvre was ruled out. Of the total bomber force of 115, sixteen were shot down, a loss rate of 14 per cent. Of those left, about half of the aircraft had sustained significant battle damage that would take precious time to repair or otherwise be written off completely. This was not a sustainable attrition rate.

It was July 1943 and the Pointblank directive, the attritional destruction of the Luftwaffe prior to D-Day, began. RAF heavy bomber squadrons, including support squadrons, crucially the newly formed RAF Mosquito Pathfinders, and supported by the USAAF, were ordered to commence at 'maximum effort'. Thousand-bomber raids were to become a reality.

Large scale raids commenced, notably the infamous Schweinfurt 'ball-bearing' raids. They were costly in aircrew and machines. They were condemned by Arthur Harris as 'typical panacea targets'. He argued that if we could work out that these were targets that could cripple German machine production, the Germans would have worked it out too, and done something to mitigate the vulnerability. The Schweinfurt raids, commencing in August 1943, did much damage but production was set to recover rapidly. Harris had a point. On the first raid, of 370 bombers, sixty were shot down, a loss rate of 17 per cent and 600 aircrew were killed or captured. More aircraft limped back to base so badly mauled that they had to undergo time-consuming major repairs. Many were scrapped altogether, again effectively increasing the loss rate. The raid had been a failure and the B-17s would have to go back again. The damage to the bomber force had been so severe that the necessary immediate follow up raid was not possible. When they did mount another raid two months later, the awaited long-range escort Mustangs had still not arrived, and the losses on the second raid were even worse. This was the point, October 1943, at which unescorted, long-range bombing raids were suspended for four months to await the arrival of the new escort fighters.

Air Chief Marshal Arthur Harris still attempted to persuade General Ira Eaker to have his fliers join up with the RAF in night bombing. Although the two men were firm friends, General Eaker was not going to budge on that one and had taken the precaution of making an appeal directly to Winston

Churchill, based on the need for daylight bombing to achieve the devastating accuracy that was much more difficult to achieve at night. Churchill was unconvinced. But General Eaker read the Prime Minster right. The prospect of round-the-clock attacks did the trick – that had strong appeal to Churchill. Henceforth, the fighting crews of the 8th AAF, after a troubled night's sleep, sometimes no sleep at all, could expect to be aroused in the early hours and invited cordially to re-engage with the terror of the day job. A slow climb towards 25,000ft, a seemingly endless cruise locked in a massive aerial machine-gun formation a mere few feet away from two other heavy-bombers' wingtips. Literally no room for manoeuvre.

Arthur Harris, commanding RAF Bomber Command, continued doing what he wanted to do, which was bombing German industrial targets at night, as an almost exclusive priority. It would not be true to say he ignored the directive to destroy Luftwaffe aircraft in battle. But he lent little in the way of support from his heavy-bomber fleets until he received a pointed reminder from Supremo Dwight Eisenhower about what his priorities should now be in the run-up to Operation Overlord. Curtis LeMay, of the USAAC so called 'Bomber Mafia' remained an arch proponent of the view that wars could and should be won by strategic bombing alone. General Carl Spaatz, a coming force, adopted a practical agnosticism on the point. But Ira Eaker seemed genuinely to have set aside Douhet strategic theory and to have embraced the conviction that bringing down Nazi Germany was best done with a massive integrated air-sea-ground approach, and that destroying the enemy's fighter-driven air superiority had to be a precursor to everything. That included strategic bombing playing a part in the destruction of aircraft factories and oil refineries deep within Germany. Most immediately, it meant long-range fighter escorts.

Casablanca brought a change of strategic prioritisation and the way the Allies would fight the war. There would be an integrated, armed-forces strategy. The idea that strategic bombing alone could win the war fell away for practical planning purposes. The strategic priority now moved to defeating the Luftwaffe in battle, not just keeping them from shooting down bombers. Rendering them incapable of significant interference with Operation Overlord, the planned seaborne invasion of northwest Europe, was to be the first priority. Mass air attacks against a seaborne invasion would almost certainly have brought about horrendous loss of soldiers' lives, so achieving air superiority was an absolute goal. This had been emphasised and foretold in the mounting of preparatory operations such as the Dieppe Raid. Daylight bombing was not being abandoned – far from it – but for the time being it became a means to a more immediate end. Gradually, the 'bombers alone' school lost traction. In particular, an increasing volume of statistical evidence indicated that losses of unescorted bombers averaged seven times as high as when escorted by fighters – devastating by any standard – and impossible to ignore. Missions beyond the inadequate, escort radius of action of Thunderbolts, as stated, were suspended.

Allied heavy bombers, henceforth, were to be escorted by long-range fighters throughout the full duration of daylight raids. From October 1943, all P-51 Merlin Mustangs produced, now the only real contender for these missions, were to be directed to the 8th AAF for this purpose.

The fighter group designated to commence bomber escort missions started working up. The first operational escort sortie was a short-range B-17 raid against Amiens, which passed without incident. More practice took place. Then came the awaited day. On 13 December 1943, Merlin Mustangs of 354th Fighter Group provided top cover escorting B-17s in a long-range attack on the harbours at Kiel. This would have taken them north-east from England around to the north of the Friesian Islands, across Schleswig-Holstein north of Hamburg, to Kiel, and then back to their bases, a round trip of over 1,400 miles. It must have been a red-letter day for the bomber crews. On this mission, their 'Little Friends' did not turn back and go home half-way along the outbound leg, leaving them to face alone the horrors in front of them. They stayed with them to the target, above them over the target, fought down the opposition whenever it arrived, and stayed with them all the way back home. Of course, there still were losses, both fighters and bombers, but these quickly became fractional. Things had surely changed.

Raids were still concentrated on disrupting aircraft production and supply facilities in Germany, primarily that of fighters, before the finished products could be used against the Allies. The first beneficiaries of this suppression were the Allied bombers themselves. It was still a slugging match, but the USAAF had been given a way of doubling its returns. It was now a war of attrition on more than equal terms. A joint raid of bombers with fighter top cover did more than bomb a few installations at high loss to its own force. Bomb-aiming with reduced enemy fighter interference had a much-increased chance of hitting targets and therefore inflicting genuine strategic damage to Germany. At the same time, it drastically reduced bomber losses. A better raid today with much fewer and sustainable losses implied a bigger and better raid tomorrow and each day that followed. The advantage was strategically accumulative.

For the Luftwaffe, this scenario was a zero-sum game. They now had to fight their way through a screen of top-class, fighter escorts before they could get to what was important – protecting Germany by shooting down the bombers. One lesson that the 8th did apply was learned, perhaps, from the mistake made by Reichsmarschall Herman Goering in the Battle of Britain in 1940. Exasperated by the losses inflicted on his bomber fleets by the RAF, he admonished his fighter leaders, ordering them to stay close to the bomber formations. This restricted his fighters' ability to take advantage of the all-important high-altitude, up-sun, high-speed diving attack – a curious mistake given that Goering himself was a former fighter pilot. The USAAF Mustang tactic was now to protect the bombers from high above them, waiting to stoop from a speed and height advantage as soon as the Luftwaffe fighters appeared, possibly and vulnerably, still in the climb. This frame of mind put the

P-51s into a strategically defensive role – clearing the way for the bombers to strike.

Then, a new commander of 8th Fighter Command arrived and put his fighter force also firmly on the strategically offensive. His name was Lieutenant General James Doolittle. 'Jimmy Doolittle' was a legend in his own lunch time. He was the commander who had flown a squadron of Mitchell B-25 medium bombers from the deck of USS aircraft carrier *Hornet* to deliver the first strike on Japan. His targets were industrial sites in Tokyo and elsewhere. This was a high-risk, special operation using drastically lightened B-25s to get them off the carrier. To pull up the nosewheel and get airborne from the deck of the *Hornet*, turned into wind, they had to have an airspeed that was within five miles per hour of the stall speed. All sixteen aircraft of the then Lieutenant Colonel Doolittle's squadron made it. They caused no significant damage to their targets but that did not matter. This was a gauntlet thrown down. This was sending a message to the Japanese; the same as was sent to Berliners. You cannot rely on distance to make you impervious. We will, eventually, find a big way to reach you. In the climb away after the raid, every aircraft commander had to make his own choice about where he would go. All but one of the B-25s were destroyed in crashes, ditching in the sea, or were abandoned by parachute. One made it to, and landed in, Vladivostok in the Soviet Union. Eight men were captured by Japanese forces in eastern China. Three of them were taken to Tokyo and publicly executed by firing squad. The Chinese people hid and sheltered many of the crews and, in the hunt for them, it is estimated that Japanese troops murdered 250,000 civilians.

The now Lieutenant General Jimmy Doolittle, made sure all his pilots were briefed that their primary function was to destroy Luftwaffe fighters. He told his squadron commanders that he required his Mustang pilots to go hunting for 'Jerries'. He hoped for, and got, a critical change of attitude. Don't focus on the bombers. Shoot down fighters whenever you encounter them and you will fulfil both objectives at the same time.

The fighter battles over Germany during the concentrated bombing of aircraft factories, battles of attrition, brought down the Luftwaffe. It was the battles between the fighters themselves that were key rather than the bombing of aircraft factories. Some 157 battle-hardened Luftwaffe pilots were killed and were replaced by young men with hardly any battle experience at all, and after an increasingly abbreviated basic training. They proved no match for the 8th AAF's Mustangs. The new kids on the block went at it and fought the opposition to a standstill. It was bloody and terrifying, but the Merlin Mustangs and the 8th's fighter pilots did their job.

There can be no report of these day-after-day fighter battles with their full-throttle, strap-hanging dives, high 'g' spine-crunching turns, desperately trying to get a fighter into your gunsight, the reek and thundering roar of your cannons firing, without mention of the Tuskegee boys. They gained a reputation that was saluted by all. The USAAF was racially segregated. Black boys were not allowed to become fighter pilots with white boys. It was decided to form an all-black pilot fighter wing. The Tuskegee were a thousand airmen who punched way above their weight as fighter pilots. The tails of their Merlin Mustangs were painted maroon, and they gained the nickname of 'Red Tails'. Bomber crews would often ask specifically for Red Tails to escort them on a raid. From Fortress crews, you could not ever get a better and more sincere compliment than that. They were noted for their nonchalant aggressiveness. It is reported that after flying a six-hour escort mission, and having seen their 'Big Friends' safe home, they still had enough fuel left to drop down low level over north-west Europe to strafe an airfield or two for good measure. Like you do. They didn't seem to understand what flight fatigue was.

The killing of experienced veterans, Luftwaffe fighter pilots, proved critical. Not the supply of aircraft. It was battle hardened pilots, not machines. This left everything open to air attack. Berliners who, throughout the war, had felt secure behind the long distances from western-based Allied warplanes, found themselves now terribly vulnerable. Goering had boasted that no bomb would land on German soil, yet Berlin was under attack by day and by night. Goering also said that the day he saw Mustangs over Berlin, he knew Germany would lose the war. He was a man of many faults, but strategic logic was not one of them. The debate about fighter escorts had been settled by the astounding air-battle successes achieved by the fighting and range capabilities of the Merlin Mustang.

This story is one of two embattled doctrines. The tactical one was whether armed bombers could be effective without a fighter escort or not. That was convincingly settled. But what of the strategic debate? Could strategic bombing alone win the war as opposed to integrated combined operations? The case of Operation Gomorrah may be instructive.

Operation Gomorrah was the reduction of Hamburg by bombing. Why Gomorrah? After the war, it became standard operating procedure to select the names of operations by random computer choice, to obviate any possibility of the selected name giving an inadvertent hint as to its objectives. Not so in the Second World War, when giving a clue seemed desirable. Perhaps this was to help dazed, sleep-deprived officers to remember what it was they were supposed to be working on today. Gomorrah was a Biblical city that, according to the book of Genesis, was destroyed by the vengeance of God for the wickedness of its people. It was destroyed by a firestorm from the sky. If German intelligence, or even Luftwaffe fighter control had caught wind of this codeword, it would not have been too difficult to guess what such a simple parable meant. Too late to do anything about it.

Hamburg was a city of two million people and the biggest port in Europe. In July 1943, RAF Bomber Command and the USAAF bombed the city for four days and three nights continuously. It was the biggest tonnage of bombs dropped in a single raid of the war so far. The 8th AAF went for the U-boat yards and aircraft factories, while the RAF attacked the city itself. The RAF concentrated as many bombers as possible (7–800) over the target in as short a time as possible to overwhelm the civil defences, and they used incendiaries as well as high explosive. This gave rise to a new phenomenon – the firestorm. Superheated air rises rapidly, pulling in more oxygenated air from below which can accelerate to hurricane strength over a very large area. It is not possible to survive this, even underground. 65,000 people were asphyxiated or burned to death. A flat, official announcement from the RAF stated, 'The city of Hamburg is now in ruins'.

Yet Hamburg, like the mythical Phoenix, did rise from the flames. Air Chief Marshal Harris, Air Officer Commanding Royal Air Force Bomber Command, had crossed it off his list as out of the war and turned his attentions to doing the same to other German cities. Given this respite, within six months Hamburg was back to three quarters of its former war productivity in some sectors, something the Allies deemed incredible at the time. The pinpoint bombing of the 8th too, had returned inconclusive results. The U-boat yards were back at work, as were the aero-engine plants. Within a few months, there emerged an increasing feeling that despite the round-the-clock bombing, the Combined Bombing Offensive (CBO), had not achieved what Douhet theorists like Harris and LeMay had predicted. The disruption of the German industrial war machine with high explosive and incendiary weapons, despite inflicting hell on the poor below, had not ended the war on its own.

To do that, the horrors of Hamburg, Essen, Lubeck, Dresden, Berlin and many other cities had to be repeated even more spectacularly. Finally, with the advance of weapon technology, maybe the 'Bomber Mafia' had the last word after all. The Second World War ended, and the world changed, in August 1945.

It took only two bombs.

Chapter 11

Epilogue

The rise of the P-51 Mustang, eventually sweeping all before it to become the only truly strategic single engine fighter of the Second World War, is like a big screen thriller. It could have gone wrong at so many points, but this Cinderella of a fighter came up with the right combination of qualities just in time to fit the bill and win its place in history. It is a story of design, manufacturing flexibility and organisational cooperation that would alter the optimisation of a machine to carry through the tasks asked of it. And far more, no matter how seemingly diverse. When, at long last, its potential was realised, it became almost heroic, if a machine can be so.

However, there is a curious footnote to the story of the desperate hunt to find a top-class single engine fighter with sufficient radius of action to fly a full mission escort defending long range bombers. In the event there was only one. But there could have been two.

The USAAF persistently asked the RAF to provide Spitfire escorts. RAF Fighter Command under Air Marshal Trafford Leigh-Mallory responded that their fighters could be used only defensively because they were range limited and not capable of escort duties. This was received Fighter Command doctrine and as was so often the case, above challenge. Both Air Marshal Harris of RAF Bomber Command, and Air Marshal Slessor of RAF Coastal Command, had also asked for Spitfire escorts for their strike aircraft. Fighter Command had responded that conversion of the Spitfire to achieve the radius of action required was simply not possible. They did not have a fighter with the range of a bomber. The response must be suspect because there was already a modified photo-reconnaissance version of the Spitfire that rivalled the Mustang in both range and fighting performance, although the reconnaissance Spitfire was not required to carry heavy guns.

US General 'Hap' Arnold therefore asked if the RAF would place its Mustang squadrons under the command of the 8th to escort his Fortresses on daylight raids alongside the 8th's own Mustangs. This request went up to Air Chief Marshal Charles Portal, Chief of the Air Staff, who offered four such squadrons, which was derisory.

Things got pointed. Arnold snapped back that Portal had 1,600 fighters under his command, and he was under-using their capabilities by restricting them to tactical and defensive duties. He cited, not his Mustangs, but his Thunderbolts, which had been modified with long range fuel tanks and were doing offensive escort work hundreds of miles out from England even though they had an unmodified range less than that of the Spitfire. He was implying that if the Spitfire was given extra tankage, it could be used on escort duties. Portal and Leigh-Mallory did not budge, Leigh-Mallory repeating that he needed all his fighters for tactical use.

Arnold decided to make a fresh approach. Portal was asked by an emissary if two single Spitfires only could be assigned to the USAAF. They would try to convert them for long-range escort duties entirely at their expense, trial them to establish their range performance and deliver them to the test pilot establishment at RAF Boscombe Down for verification. The two Spits (both Mk IXs, the latest operational variant) were given over and shipped across to the States to have the work carried out. By spring 1944 the two aircraft had been modified and initial testing proved that they now had the radius of action required for very long-range strategic bomber escort work. They were being readied for shipping back when someone had an idea. Instead of shipping them back, why not fly them back to England from the US? That would make the point impressively. It was done. Boscombe Down tested them and verified the figures.

Then, something mysterious happened. Nothing. The conversions to long range Spitfires were approved, but only six months later, by which time *Operation Pointblank* had achieved its objectives. The Luftwaffe was a spent force and Germany would be defeated. Allied air forces were never to have the strategic benefit of long-range escort Spitfires.